Hope you enjoy this
book.
Every good wish

Caroline

087 9694837

The Art of

ASKING THE
RIGHT QUESTIONS

A People Manager's Toolkit

CAROLINE McENERY

Published by OAK TREE PRESS
Cork, Ireland
www.oaktreepress.com / www.SuccessStore.com

© 2017 Caroline McEnery

A catalogue record of this book is available from the British Library.

ISBN 978 1 78119 271 9 (Hardback)
ISBN 978 1 78119 272 6 (Paperback)
ISBN 978 1 78119 273 3 (ePub)
ISBN 978 1 78119 274 0 (Kindle)
ISBN 978 1 78119 275 7 (PDF)

Illustrations © JR Casas / Adobe Stock Photos
Cover design: Kieran O'Connor Design

CONTENTS

SECTION 3: MAXIMISING YOUR POTENTIAL

ACKNOWLEDGEMENTS

There are so many people I need to thank along the journey of writing this book, which is a culmination of my experience, education and life lessons. Wow! Have *I* enjoyed that journey! I feel really privileged to do a job I love with such a great team and such a great customer base every day.

I'd like to start my Thank Yous with my team at The HR Suite, both past and present. I so appreciate all your contribution and the way you always go the extra mile. I'm genuinely indebted to you all. Thank you all from the bottom of my heart for your support, professionalism, positivity and continuous improvement attitude that we keep raising the bar for our customers and enjoy the journey as a team along the way.

I've had the privilege of working with amazing people along my career journey, so I really want to thank my colleagues, managers and mentors both in Kerry Group and the Garvey Group. You all pushed me to be better, and to strive for more. I learnt so much and enjoyed every minute. Thank you.

Paula Fitzsimons from Going for Growth and ACORNS has always been so supportive in my entrepreneurship journey that I'm delighted to be a lead entrepreneur of ACORNS, helping great women grow great businesses. Paula, you are genuinely an inspiration and I appreciate all you've done for me. To my lead entrepreneurs and Going for Growth peers who I'm thrilled to call my friends: Wow, ladies, what a superb network I'm privileged to be part of that really drives me and my business both personally and professionally. Thank you for your support and friendship.

I'd also like to particularly thank Tomas Hayes and Fiona Leahy from the Kerry LEO and Julie Sinnamon, Jean O'Sullivan and

Sarita Johnson from Enterprise Ireland. Without their support, this journey would have been so much more challenging. Thank you all.

I'd like to thank all our loyal customers that we've had the privilege to work with. I so appreciate that you trust us with your HR and your people. Your support and business is genuinely appreciated. You are such fantastic ambassadors for our business and give us the highest compliment we could ever wish for through your ongoing referrals. Thank you for your trust, your business and support.

I'd like to thank my amazing publisher, Brian O'Kane of Oak Tree Press, for his input, belief and expertise. Brian, you were first class and an absolute pleasure to work with.

Finally, I'd like to thank my amazing family and friends. I'm so lucky to have so many people in my life that are such a positive influence and really believe in me and support me in everything I do. They make my ordinary extraordinary. They support me when I need a 'phone a friend' and help to celebrate the successes and achievements along the way. I realise I'm so lucky to have each and every one of you in my life and thank you sincerely for your support.

I'm a big believer in enjoying the journey. The culmination of all the people who've influenced me along the way means I get to do what I love with amazing people every day. Thank you all. Without each and every one of you, this book would not be possible. I hope you enjoy it as much as I have enjoyed writing it.

Caroline McEnery, The HR Suite

INTRODUCTION

The Cloths of Heaven

Had I the heavens' embroidered cloths,
Enwrought with golden and silver light,
The blue and the dim and the dark cloths
Of night and light and the half-light,
I would spread the cloths under your feet:
But I, being poor, have only my dreams;
I have spread my dreams under your feet;
Tread softly because you tread on my dreams.

WB Yeats

This wonderful poem by WB Yeats is one of my favourites. It always reminds me that, when working with and managing people, you are dealing with people's dreams and hopes.

Since work is completely entangled in all our lives, you must tread softly in your dealings with all employees and colleagues.

Ask the right questions at the right time

A lot of the HR advice, mentoring and training tips I give to business owners and managers hinges on ensuring you **ask the right questions at the right time** and then listen, silently and carefully, so you can then identify how best you should progress proactively to the next steps from there.

This book should be on your desk as a 'go to guide' that you can dip into as needed to remind you of the key questions you should ask in different situations throughout the employment journey. By asking the right questions, you will enhance your team's skills to maximise their own talent and you will make your business or department more successful by engaging your team's knowledge and skills. This book is a summary of our top tips to help make your journey of people management run more smoothly so you can maximise your very best resource – your team.

Your team deserves the best manager you can be

I have included a personal action plan review at the end of the book to help you self-assess your own skills and current management techniques. Hopefully, you will identify some tips to enhance your skills – I know from the experience of other managers that they really do work! Enjoy the journey!

2 QUESTIONING

Questions are the best way to move from what you don't know to what you need to know.

There are lots of reasons you might ask a question in the employment context – for example, to help unstick employees, to signpost our team, to mentor and coach, to gather information … the list goes on.

But, before you ask a question of an employee, you need to ask yourself a few questions to ensure you are on the right track.

The right question; the right time; the right place; the right context

First, **ask yourself whether you are the right person to ask this question** to get the desired information or result. If you are not, then pass the baton to the person who is.

Second, it is really important to ask the **right question**. If you ask the wrong question, you risk getting the wrong answer or perhaps you will find that you do not have enough information to proactively progress to the next step, whatever that might be.

Last, it is also important to ask yourself whether you are asking the question **at the right time, in the right way**. Throughout this book, you will see different scenarios that show the importance of timing and of using emotional intelligence.

Checking that you are the right person, asking the right question at the right time in the right way will make your job as a people manager so much easier, since you will get the full benefit from every question that you ask.

Let's look at an example.

> Megan has just come in late and looks very flustered. It's not her first time being late so, as her manager, you know you need to discuss her attendance with her.
>
> ### Scenario 1
>
> You walk over to Megan's desk and say, "Why are you late again? You know that's not acceptable". Megan shouts back at you, "You don't care why I am late. Leave me alone to get on with my job". You are shocked and don't know what to do.
>
> ### Scenario 2
>
> You acknowledge Megan's arrival with a simple "Good morning". Then, from your desk, you send Megan an email, asking her to pop in to your office after tea break as you would like to have a chat with her.
>
> When she comes into your office, you make some small talk before asking, "Megan, how are things with you?". You listen and wait for her to answer.
>
> Then you highlight that you are concerned as you have noticed she has been late a few mornings recently, which is not like her, and you ask, "Is there anything I can do to help you?" Again, you wait and listen carefully to her reply.
>
> You reiterate that she is a valued member of the team but that the business requires her to be at her desk at 9am to answer the customers' calls. You remind her that and you are available to help support her in any way you can to ensure she is at work on

time and that hopefully she will trust you to tell you what is going on so you can help address the root of the problem and come up with a mutually acceptable solution.

How you ask your questions is very important. If you ask in a blaming tone or with a raised voice, the employee automatically will be defensive. Instead you need to remain calm and objective. If you do so, the employee is much more likely to mirror your tone and professionalism as you take the heat out of the situation and highlight your purpose clearly and calmly.

Using the rationale of the requirements of the business depersonalises the situation and helps the employee to see an objective reason for your request.

When you talk to your team in a non-emotive context and in a private setting, you are much more likely to have a constructive conversation. In contrast, scenario 1 was in public and Megan was flustered, so she was emotional, and as a result the situation spiralled into something more complex to deal with. Remember that your role as manager is always to turn down the heat and to nip issues in the bud.

The timing of the conversation is important. Nothing is so urgent that you cannot wait until you have thought through the right approach to take. If you rush a conversation and let your emotions get involved, you might regret what you asked, when you asked it, how you asked it or where you asked it.

If in doubt say, "We need to discuss this further. But let's do it in the afternoon" rather than reacting at the time. You can then think through what you need to know, what you need to ask to help you find that out and what outcome you want to achieve - and then plan your approach.

Always give praise in public but only give constructive feedback in private. Where necessary, 'press pause' and reschedule the meeting until later. Park a contentious matter at a team meeting by saying, "We will schedule a specific meeting about that later but let's park it for now". This allows you to turn down the heat and take time to plan your approach.

Asking the right question will be positive and productive and give you the information you need or the result you desire. Your questions need to be thought-provoking and to encourage the recipient to think about their answer.

If you ask the wrong question, you will get the wrong information – hence the importance of thinking through your approach.

Let's look at an example.

Scenario 1

"Johnny, do you like working with customers?"

Scenario 2

"Johnny, tell me about a specific time you had to deal with a difficult customer complaint and the steps you took to resolve it?"

In scenario 1, you know that Johnny is going to tell you that he loves customers – he is going to tell you what he thinks you want to hear.

In scenario 2, you asked Johnny to tell us about a specific example and the steps he took – this is much more difficult to bluff. Always give the person lots of time to give you as much detail as possible. This will give you a real insight into what the employee would do in a real-life customer relations situation in the future. And it will trigger further probing questions also.

Types of questions

There are many types of questions, including

* ❖ **Leading** questions, which simply put words into the other person's mouth – effectively asking them to tell you what you want to hear.

* ❖ **Multiple** questions, which generally confuse the person who is required to answer them, so they answer the question that's easiest for them or shows them in the best light – not very helpful if you need to know the answer for the other question(s).

* ❖ **Closed** questions, which generally get a "Yes" or a "No" reply and so are best suited to specific information-gathering situations or to confirm information – for example, "Did you book the meeting room for 1pm?"

* ❖ **Open** questions, which require more than a one-word reply and generally result in a broad reply that both gathers information and gives you an insight into the topic from the employee's perspective.

The right questions to ask are generally open questions. They include "What?", "Why?" or "How?" questions. Personally, I find "Why?" and "How?" questions and are the most useful – perhaps it's because they are most thought-provoking that they elicit the best information.

Examples of open questions include:

> **Tell me about a time that you encountered a very difficult customer?**
>
> **What did you do next?**
>
> **Why did you do that?**
>
> **How did you persuade the customer to accept that offer?**

These **open questions** are key to helping you to maximise your employee's potential and to coach them proactively.

Questions are the best way to move from what you don't know to what you need to know.

I find that a question like "What are the available options?" is great for getting the full information regarding a situation and the possible solutions available to solve the issue. It helps the employee to understand the problem themselves and to come up with the options themselves. This ensures that they are developing their knowledge and problem-solving skills, thus empowering them. Otherwise, if you give them all the answers, you will find that you are not just doing your own job but also doing theirs as they will come to you any time they have a problem.

Encourage curiosity, blue sky thinking, brainstorming and solution-focused problem-solving by asking the right questions. Think of how many questions small children ask. They're so curious and want to learn continuously. You need to get your team – and yourself – thinking outside the box by asking them the right thought-provoking questions. Blue sky thinking encourages asking questions with no barriers – that's what you need your employees to do more often. And, through your guidance, *via* asking great questions, it can become a reality.

This is really important in business development and in focusing on identifying improvements – for example, ask yourself:

> **If we remove the current barriers, what's possible? The sky is the limit.**
>
> **What are the customer's real pain points and how can we solve that problem for them?**

Useful questions

Here are some useful questions for your tool kit that will come in handy in a variety of situations throughout the employment journey.

TO CLARIFY

What happened exactly?

Just to be clear, I hear .... Is that what you are saying?

TO CHECK ALL IS OK

I am just checking in to see how things are going with you?

You don't seem to be yourself. We are concerned for you. Are you OK?

Can we do anything to help support you?

Please ask if you need anything.

TO FACT-FIND

Can you take me through the steps of what happened and who was involved? Be as specific as you can.

TO GET A HELICOPTER VIEW

Let's take a step back and look at the full picture of what we are trying to achieve. Now can you give me your opinion?

What are the key issues?

What is the overarching requirement?

TO PROBLEM-SOLVE

What is the specific problem?

What are your options?

What are the pros and cons of each option?

What is the best option?

Will that solve your problem on time / on budget, etc?

Have you any other concerns / issues?

TO HELP GET SOMEONE UNSTUCK

How do you think we can solve that problem?

What is the end objective?

What are the steps you need to take to reach that objective?

What are your SMART (specific, measurable, achievable, realistic and time-bound) goals to get there?

What are the obstacles along the way?

What do you need to do first to get started on the journey to get there?

TO FOCUS ON THE FUTURE

OK, now we have assessed the issues you need to improve, let's draw a line in the sand. What are you going to do differently going forward?

What support do you need?

When can I expect to see that change implemented?

TO TURN DOWN THE HEAT AND CONTROL EMOTIONS

I think this is what you are saying ... Am I hearing you correctly?

Be assured I hear your perspective. Is there anything else you want to add?

TO PROVIDE A RATIONALE

The business requires you to ...

I am a believer in 'short and sweet' but make sure always that your goals are **SMART: specific, measurable, achievable, realistic and time-bound.** Think of the result you want to achieve; focus on this in your questioning; and follow-up afterwards.

So, to summarise, you can see that asking the right questions can have benefits in any organisation. In this book, we look specifically at the employment journey but developing your questioning and listening skills will have far-reaching benefits for you and your overall career and, in turn, for your organisation.

Top tips

❖ **Ask yourself whether you are the best person to ask this question to get the required information / result.**

❖ **Take time out and 'press pause' if you are not prepared or are out of your depth.**

❖ **Turn down the heat and control emotions.**

❖ **Nip issues in the bud.**

❖ **Prepare for the conversation.**

❖ **What is the right question to get the required information / result based on the goal?**

❖ **What is the best context, timing and setting?**

❖ **Use "the business requires ...." as a rationale.**

❖ **Ask open questions - for example, "What?", "Why?" and "How?"**

❖ **Use blue sky thinking and open questions for business development and to maximise your employee's ideas.**

LISTENING

The more you listen, the clearer your understanding becomes.

The key to asking the right question is waiting for the answer - and being patient enough to get the full answer. That's not as easy as it sounds.

Be patient and listen

Although listening is a key people management skill, managers often find it easier to answer an employee's problem rather than to ask the right questions to help unstick, signpost, mentor and coach them. Whether this is due to time constraints or simply because the manager thinks it doesn't matter: **if you don't listen, you are not getting the full picture, you are not fully engaging your team and you are not developing your team.** Three good reasons to listen!

The importance of giving the employee the opportunity to be heard cannot be overstated. You also need to emphasise that you want to hear what they have to say fully - only then can you move to the next step.

You need to prepare yourself to listen during these sessions with employees because it's too easy to feel you haven't the time to listen or you are just not in the zone to listen. If you don't listen, it is no longer a two-way conversation. You will not get the full benefit from your interaction and it is unlikely the employee will either - both of you lose out. So you need to practice being ready to listen and be silent and to invest the time and effort required to hone this key management skill. You will reap the rewards from your investment, trust me!

A key requirement is to ensure you have enough time available to give the process the time it deserves. Because you won't feel rushed to give an answer yourself or to move on too quickly without giving the employee a full opportunity to respond, this will encourage you to listen more effectively to get the information you need to move the process on. Also:

- ❖ Try to maintain eye contact and show the employee you are fully attentive and present to give the communication process the time it deserves.

- ❖ Always try to put your employee at ease - you'll get more out of them if they are more relaxed.

- ❖ Avoid distractions - if that's not possible, reschedule the meeting as it's not fair to the employee and it's not of real value to the organisation.

A powerful question to ask is "What's going on for you?" But it is only powerful if you listen and let the employee answer it. It is also really important to check the "Why?"

Let me give you an example.

Joanne has not been performing in her role lately and has been making lots of mistakes. It's not like her; she used to be a great employee. You have scheduled a performance meeting with her, so let's look at two scenarios that could result from different approaches you might take. Remember that your goal is to ensure Joanne's performance improves.

Scenario 1

You bring Joanne into your office and ask her why she is making so many mistakes. You explain that she needs to concentrate more or it will result in disciplinary action. Joanne cries at this news and she leaves the meeting promising to do better.

Scenario 2

You ask Joanne, "How are things with you at the moment?" and you pause to listen carefully to what she says.

She says, "Not too bad".

You remain silent for a while and see that she is reluctant to say any more. So you ask, "Does that mean they are not good?"

You explain, "I don't want to pry but I am concerned for you as you have been with the company a long time and are a great employee".

Joanne then explains that she is going through a difficult time currently due to personal circumstances.

You ask, "What can we do to help you?" and again to pause to listen and let her think about what support she needs.

She asks for a later start two mornings a week.

You explain that her working hours need to be in line with business requirements but you are willing to see if this arrangement works on a trial period if it would really help her situation. You explain that you need her to monitor her own accuracy and attention to detail more carefully as the business requirements are to ensure all the accounts are up-to-date and correct. Joanne acknowledges this and thanks you for your help and understanding.

The difference between the two scenarios highlights the importance of asking the right question, listening carefully and giving the employee a chance to think and reply. Sometimes that may require a follow-up meeting.

Good listeners:

❖ Do not accept everything the employee tells them at face value – they probe the why.

❖ Ask open questions that are specific and relevant.

❖ Are patient - wait for the other person to answer.

❖ Don't interrupt - listen - remember twice as much listening as talking.

❖ Let the employee finish before asking the next question.

❖ Avoid distractions and give the employee time.

❖ Clarify understanding and what was agreed.

The more you listen, the clearer your understanding becomes.

Barriers to listening

Be aware of the potential barriers that might prevent you listening effectively. They include:

❖ Lack of preparation and a desire to stay in control.

❖ Lack of objectivity – you have decided what to do next.

❖ Lack of empathy.

❖ Lack of time or concentration.

❖ Lack of patience – you know the answer and want to give it.

Use clarifying questions

You can use clarifying questions in two ways:

- ❖ To ensure you are clear on what you have heard to avoid any ambiguity.

- ❖ To ensure you and the employee are clear on what was said and agreed.

For example, you might say, "So to be clear, what I heard was …. Is that right?" or you might ask "Can you tell me more about that to ensure I fully understand it?"

By paraphrasing what was said to ensure clarity and by being fully present, you show you are fully engaged in this very important employee meeting.

Body language

What is not said often says as much as what is said. Body language and tone of voice offers an additional insight to the words being said, which may change their meaning entirely. You need to be attentive and fully engaged to notice this underlying message.

Questions and listening are powerful skills in your toolkit to becoming a proactive manager. In the coming chapters, we will assess the best questions at each stage of the people management journey to help you when you need some top tips.

Top tips

- ❖ **Ask the question and be silent to listen; don't be afraid of the silence.**

- ❖ **You have two ears and one mouth, so do twice as much listening as talking.**

- ❖ **The importance of giving the employee the opportunity to be heard can't be overstated.**

- ❖ **Give the process the time it deserves.**

- ❖ **Ask open questions.**

- ❖ **Ask clarifying / probing questions as required to ensure you have all the information you need.**

- ❖ **Watch for body language - learn to read it.**

4 PAPER TRAILS

If you can't prove it, it never happened!

Don't underestimate the importance of keeping notes - a 'paper trail' - of the key points discussed and agreed at meetings. This will ensure everyone is clearly on the same page and prevents grey areas, full of ambiguity, that always cause further difficulty down the road.

It is good practice to send a follow-up email to confirm what was agreed to ensure both you and the employee are on the same page going forward.

Communication

Remember that we all communicate and remember differently. Research conducted by The Master Trainer Institute highlights that people's preferences for how they receive communication were:

- ❖ Auditory / Hearing = 7%
- ❖ Visual / Seeing = 51%
- ❖ Kinaesthetic / Feeling / Doing = 42%

This research also confirmed that the likelihood of remembering the communication correctly 24 hours later also differs by form of communication:

- ❖ Auditory = 38%
- ❖ Visual = 81%
- ❖ Kinaesthetic = 77%

So this emphasises the importance of not only **telling** the employee what you want to tell them but also **visually following up** and **getting them involved** in doing it themselves.

Clarity is key

Often managers skirt around an issue so much that neither manager nor employee are clear afterwards about the message. Be clear, avoid ambiguity - then everyone knows where they stand.

For example, here's an email you might send to an employee after a performance meeting:

> Thanks, Megan, for taking the time to meet me today regarding your performance.
>
> I am glad we agreed that you will address the current concerns regarding accuracy. We will meet again in two weeks to assess this improvement, as we really need to ensure all the work in your department is 100% accurate consistently.
>
> In the interim we have agreed to facilitate you to start at 10am on Tuesday and Thursday on a trial basis in line with business requirements.
>
> If you have any queries, let me know. Otherwise, we will meet again on the 12th at 4pm as agreed.

Remember keep it simple; ensure it's clear and SMART - specific, measurable, achievable; realistic and time-bound.

Email is time- and date-stamped so it's the best form of a paper trail record but you can use whatever works best for you.

Remember to file it - ideally electronically (to save trees!) - so you can access it easily at any stage in the future if you need to refer back to it. What system will you use to do this? Agree it now to ensure you have it in place and ensure you use it consistently for all relevant employee records.

Prove it!

Records and your paper trail are key. Records are proof and, without a solid paper trail, you don't have any proof. **If you can't prove it, it never happened!**

When keeping records, ask yourself:

> **What was the goal I was trying to achieve?**
> **What did I ask?**
> **What did they say?**
> **What did we agree?**
> **What follow-up is required?**

Here are some examples of common processes recorded for you to show short and concise you can keep your paper trail:

Probation

Following our meeting of today, I want to confirm what was discussed and agreed in relation to your probationary review in your role as xxxx.

At the meeting, I outlined that your performance has been falling short of our required standards and we are therefore giving you an opportunity to improve. The following are the key areas where improvements need to be made following our discussion: [what is wrong] and [how to improve].

Going forward we ask that you become more aware of these areas, as a failure to improve on this will result in the failure of your probation.

Resignation

I am writing in relation to our recent conversation when you confirmed that you were resigning from your position.

Please note as discussed I would appreciate it if you can confirm this in writing for me by return email for our records.

I would like to take the opportunity to wish you every success in your new career and I will schedule an exit interview with you next week.

Should you have any questions please do not hesitate to contact me.

Data protection

As organisations increase their reliance on information and communications technology in the workplace, various matters surrounding the use of technology and data protection arise. The Data Protection Acts 1988 and 2003 aim to address the privacy issues surrounding the information about individuals held on computers. The Acts regulate the collection, processing, use of and disclosure of personal information relating to individuals. Data protection laws ensure that personal details given to organisations are kept private and safe by placing the responsibility to do so on a 'data controller' who must police the content and use of these details.

From the start of the recruitment process right through the employment journey, it is important to be aware of the obligations on you as the employer when it comes to data protection and your employees.

The Data Protection Acts 1988 and 2003 permits an individual to request and receive copies of certain information and documents an organisation holds relating to him / her. According to the Data Commissioner, data subject access requests are "fundamental rights" of individuals. Once an employee has submitted a request in writing under the Acts, the data controller must respond within 40 days. The date controller may charge for responding to such a request.

In relation to CCTV recordings, a person or employee requesting information should provide the necessary information to a data controller, such as the date, time and location of the recording. If the image is of such poor quality as not to clearly identify an individual, that image may not be considered to be personal data. In giving a person a copy of his / her data, the data controller may provide a still picture or a series of still pictures, a tape or a disk with relevant images. However, other people's images should be obscured before the data are released.

The Data Protection Acts also place obligations and responsibilities on companies and their agents – their employees – in relation to information under their care. For example:

- ❖ Reasons for decisions that you make must be documented – clearly and objectively.

- ❖ Individuals' personal details must be accurate and factual – where it is necessary to express an opinion, ensure that it is reasonable and supported by facts.

- ❖ Files must be updated with relevant information, where necessary.

- ❖ If you work for a public body such as government department, anything you write in the course of your work could be released under the Freedom of Information Acts 1997 and 2003.

The General Data Protection Regulation (GDPR) was published by the European Commission in January 2012 and adopted on 27 April 2016. The GDPR will come into force across the European Union on 25 May 2018.

HR files

The Data Protection Acts require that data are "adequate, relevant and not excessive" for the purpose for which they are collected. It is advised that employee files for those who have left your employment are retained for three years.

In addition, it is important for every organisation to limit the amount of data held on any employee. You need to ensure the data is objectively required to be held on the employee's file and is up-to-date. Note that an employee's bank details should not be kept on the employee's HR file once they have been given to payroll to process.

So you should ensure all information held on employee's files are accurate and relevant and you should not record anything you would not be in a position to give the employee a copy of.

Check what other records you need to keep in terms of your people management obligations for your team. These may include timesheets, training records, leave requests, etc.

Once you are aware of what is required, ensure you collate this information on a timely basis. Asking employees to put all their requests in writing is a great help towards your record-keeping obligations – all you need to do is to file their request, as well as your own response. Remember that if you haven't got the paper trail, it never happened.

Top tips

- ❖ **Keep your records clear, consistent and concise.**
- ❖ **Ensure your message is clear when confirming what you agreed, will do etc. - use the SMART model.**
- ❖ **If it hasn't been recorded in a paper trail, it never happened.**
- ❖ **Avoid grey areas / ambiguity at all costs.**
- ❖ **Don't record anything on an employee's file unless you would be happy to give them a copy of it.**
- ❖ **Ensure all files are accurate and factually correct.**

VALUES

**Positive affirmation makes core
values a reality.**

Core values

Your business's core values underpin your culture and are essential to your business success as they set the standard regarding what you do and how you do it – they are your guiding principles.

Ensuring all your team are clear regarding the culture and core values sets the standard for everyone; it's the way things are done in your organisation. This becomes the norm and sets the tone and personality for your company.

Ask yourself these questions:

> **How would you describe the core values currently displayed by you and your team?**
>
> **How would you like your customers / suppliers to describe their interaction with your organisation?**
>
> **How would you like your employees to describe your guiding principles of how things are done in your business and or department?**
>
> **What are the company's personality and core values?**
>
> **What do you aspire them to be?**
>
> **Can you give examples of how you and your team can live the core values with colleagues, customers, suppliers, etc?**

Identifying core values

If you haven't already done it (or haven't done it recently), identifying your core values is an excellent exercise to do with your team to clarify the company's culture and values.

Our Guiding Principles

The **Core Values** poster above will help you to capture your core values based on the questions above. Encourage all your team to honestly contribute to the discussion. Remember to listen carefully to their input and give them a chance to be heard, so as to positively reinforce the importance of their input.

For example, from the discussion, you might decide that your core values are trust, listening, curiosity, honestly, respect, innovative, positivity, customer focus, etc. Our core values at The HR Suite are shown below.

Pier 17, Dingle Road, Tralee, Co Kerry
Tel: +353 (0)66 7102887 Email: info@thehrsuiteonline.com

Let me give you **an example of how beneficial core values are**.

Matt is really negative and complains regularly about anything and everything. His colleagues are getting frustrated. During an exit interview with a staff member, you are told that that the team is not performing as a team, because of Matt's poor attitude and negativity. You were unaware of the problem. Now that you know, you need to tackle it.

Scenario 1

You bring Matt into your office and tell him, "You really need to improve your bad attitude. It's affecting the team and it won't be accepted anymore". Matt says you are picking on him and says there is no issue with his attitude. He asks you who told you this was a problem. You are compromised now as you promised the employee who left you would not say who told you about the issue. The meeting ends, with neither yourself nor Matt being happy.

Scenario 2

You confirm whether the employee will invoke the grievance procedure regarding Matt's attitude or give you a statement you can give to Matt to outline examples of the concerns in relation to his attitude. The employee agrees.

You then meet Matt and ask whether he is aware of the company's core values? Matt confirms he is and says they are positivity, integrity and customer service.

You ask if Matt feels he is displaying these core values proactively in his work and dealings with colleagues and customers as required. Matt doesn't answer but just shrugs.

You then ask him for some specific examples of when he displayed them recently. You ask him to take some time to think this through as it's really important to the organisation. You then ask the question again. Matt says he is not sure but supposes he hasn't been proactive in displaying them with his team or customers.

You outline that it is a specific business requirement of all staff working in the business that they display these core values in all their interactions and dealings and that it's not acceptable for anyone to be in conflict with these core values.

You confirm that you will meet Matt on a bi-weekly basis and will require specific examples of when and where Matt is displaying these core values proactively. Failure to do this will result in a formal performance improvement plan or ultimately disciplinary action, if no improvement is achieved. Matt acknowledges this and agrees to address his current performance. You agree the date and time of a next meeting.

You are relieved that you didn't have to use the examples the employee gave you but it was good to have them in reserve in case Matt refused to acknowledge his unacceptable behaviour.

Values build culture

Once you have agreed the core values, then get everyone to sign up to being an advocate for displaying them proactively. Make your core values part of your organisation's culture and integral to your everyday business life and dealings with all your stakeholders.

You can do this *via* team meetings, which can be backed up visually by using the **Core Values** poster. I also recommend placing this poster in a common area to remind employees of their commitment to bring these guiding principles to life and to being committed to displaying them on a continuous basis.

Remind your team of their commitment to these guiding principles and core values on a regular basis. Positively reinforce it when employees display these core values and nip it in the bud with proactive constructive discussions if people show behaviours in conflict with them. Always be an advocate for displaying the core values yourself by leading by example.

It is important that you give lots of positive reinforcement and praise and ask staff members at team meetings how they proactively advocate these core values to ensure that everyone knows they are core to the business success and are a requirement of all the team.

You need to become the "culture police". When you spot issues, nip them in the bud fast by having a constructive performance conversation regarding your concerns. Also recognise and reward people who are in tune with your core values and culture.

Recognise employee efforts in displaying these core values as much as their results and celebrate and make heroes of those who wow customers when they display these core values.

I find that over time employees also become the culture police themselves and they address other employee's behaviours if they are out of sync with the culture they become proud of. You hear them say "That's not how we do things around here …". This self-enforcement is valuable in helping your culture become integral within your company in everything you do rather than just being aspirational. What can you do to make this happen in your organisation and department?

Your company uses its core values to help it to achieve its vision, mission and objectives, both for the organisation and for each individual department. Ensure you are clear regarding the vision, mission and goals both for the organisation and for your department so all your team are clear on them also and the role they play in making them happen.

- ❖ Vision: **Where** we want to be in 5 years' time as a company – for example, the number 1 provider of xxxx in Ireland.

- ❖ Mission: **What** we are going to be famous for.

- ❖ Objectives: **How** we are going to make this happen. Be sure your objectives are SMART.

Your Core Values underpin your company's culture and how you interact and behave with all stakeholders. Positive affirmation makes these values a reality.

Top tips

- ❖ **The standard you set is the standard you get; keep raising the bar.**

- ❖ **Use a team meeting to help set your core values.**

- ❖ **Reassess them regularly to ensure everyone is walking the talk.**

- ❖ **Set these core values as the requirements of the business.**

- ❖ **Talk to employees whose performance does not proactively display and advocate these behaviours.**

- ❖ **Encourage everyone to be a member of the culture police - in particular, the managers in your team.**

- ❖ **Hero examples where these core values are displayed when staff wow the customer or team.**

- ❖ **Recognise effort as much as results.**

6 MANAGING

You need to focus on all three aspects of task, team and individual to be successful.

Often managers get promoted into people management positions accidentally, with little or no training, so take stock and assess what your role involves and what you should be managing as a people manager.

Management responsibilities

John Adair's Action Centred Leadership model illustrates his three core management responsibilities:

❖ Achieving the task.

❖ Managing and developing the team or group.

❖ Managing and developing individuals.

You need to **focus on all three aspects of task, team and individual to be successful**.

If things are off target or you hit a blip along the way, ask yourself these questions to help identify where the issue lies and to get yourself back on track again.

Ask yourself these questions:

TASK

Are the tasks smart and clear?

Have I a clear plan?

Have my employees the resources necessary to do their job?

Is there clarity of responsibility and accountability?

Is my communication and feedback clear and timely?

Are there clear standards?

Is there a process or procedure?

Am I monitoring performance against the agreed plan?

TEAM

Am I part of the culture police for the team?

Do I nip issues in the bud proactively?

Am I encouraging team cohesion?

Am I communicating to the team?

Are the team's roles clearly defined?

Has the team the right skills to achieve the goals?

INDIVIDUAL

Am I giving individual feedback?

Am I identifying training requirements?

Am I providing support and communication?

Am I giving each employee enough time to support them in achieving their tasks?

Am I maximising all the different individuals' potential fully?

Time Management

If you constantly tell yourself you haven't enough time, you will convince yourself that you don't have enough time. Instead let's look at how you can best manage the time available.

There are only 86,400 precious seconds in your day. So, to use this time effectively, it is important to be clear about what you are doing. Ask yourself:

> **What are the key areas of your job that are priorities?**
>
> **Am I the right person to be doing that task?**
>
> **Can I delegate it? If so, to whom?**
>
> **Is it an important task?**
>
> **Is there a schedule for when it will be done?**

Remember it is imperative to focus on the things that matter the most and are of most value based on importance, not just urgency. When planning tasks for the day and week, remember to do so according to their priority. The next step is to break tasks into manageable smaller mini-tasks. These mini-tasks should be spread out over your daily and weekly plan. Ensure you set realistic timeframes and review your plan throughout your working day.

Using a proven system for managing your time can help you achieve the right things at the right time, allowing you to achieve your objectives.

To manage your time well it is important to try to stick to your plan and never over-plan as interruptions will inevitably change things. Be aware that the small things you do every day are all important tasks that work towards achieving your career and business goals.

Time audit

Conducting a time audit can be useful in helping you become more efficient in the workplace. Keep a log of what you actually do each day for a few days or a week. This may show a different use of your time from what you think you are actually spending your time on. A time audit will allow you to assess whether you are spending the most time on the most important clients, tasks or otherwise. It can be an effective tool in identifying and so eliminating bad habits and work that should be done by someone else or shouldn't be done at all.

Try to use the 'right first time' principle – for every email or message, the first time you come to it either bin it, deal with it (if it will take less than two minutes to do so) or schedule it for a later time. Then do it completely at the scheduled time.

Avoid multitasking – instead, concentrate completely on getting one task fully completed before moving onto the next one, especially if the tasks require high levels of attention to detail and concentration. The more you jump from one task to another, the more time you waste getting up to speed on where you left off.

Be careful what you say "Yes" to. Do not accept a task if it is not your job - you don't have the time or resources. Be nice and helpful, but be realistic also. If you do accept a task, be honest and clear about delivery times so you manage the other person's expectations!

Procrastination

One of the biggest time wasters can be procrastination. We all know the feeling of putting things off until later but the fact remains that these jobs must get done eventually.

People who procrastinate tend to spend time on other tasks that are trivial or of no consequence - as a result, they have no time to do their more challenging and important tasks. In time, this becomes a bad habit that is difficult to get out of and affects the person's standard of work as well as his / her emotions. To combat procrastination and make a start, do something you have been putting off for a while.

Scheduling

Work to your circadian rhythm - your natural body clock energy. Many people work best in the morning, so that's when they should focus on tackling the harder tasks that require their full attention - meetings and easier work can be done in the afternoons. Work out when you are most energetic and work to maximise this time by tackling your most challenging work at this stage of the day. Effective time management increases your productivity and helps you achieve your business goals sooner rather than later.

Schedule all your tasks - if it's not scheduled, it may not get done! 50 minutes is long enough per task - then walk around to re-energise and re-oxygenate your brain so you will be refreshed and ready to tackle the next task.

Take time out every day just to give your brain a chance to think and plan - **being too busy is the biggest barrier to good time management.** Schedule this time too!

Communication

It is widely accepted, based on Professor Albert Mehrabian's research in the 1970s, that non-verbal tone and body language has a very significant impact on communication. He found that, in messages pertaining to feelings and attitudes:

❖ 7% of the message is in the words that are spoken - what is said.

❖ 38% of the message is paralinguistic - the tone or the way that the words are said.

❖ 55% of the message is in facial expression - body language.

COMMUNICATION

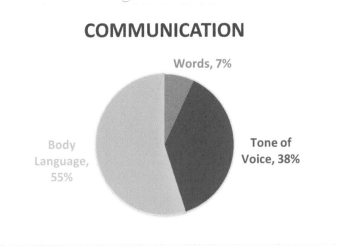

Only 7% of communication relates to what you say and 93% is how you communicate it!

So **it's important to ensure that what you meant to communicate was received as you intended.**

Asking clarifying questions and ensuring understanding are key tools to effective communication. So, at the end of a meeting or discussion, always ask the employee:

> **Can you summarise what we have agreed?**
>
> **Can you email me your understanding of what we agreed?**
>
> **Just to be clear I want to check that you understand that XXXX (be specific & paraphrase) is what we agreed.**

Also remember that employees want lots of communication so ensure you schedule regular communication updates with your team - both individually and for the team. Encourage them to come to you at any stage - make your 'open door' policy a reality!

Delegation

It's not possible to do everything yourself, so you need to ensure you delegate tasks effectively.

The key steps in delegation are:

❖ Decide on the **task** to delegate.

❖ Decide who is the right **person** to do this task.

❖ **Delegate** the task clearly and effectively using the SMART model. Clarify understanding.

❖ **Monitor progress** – "I am just checking in to see how you are getting on and whether you need any support to meet the deadline? You know where I am if you need any help!"

❖ Confirm **the task is completed** and give feedback – "Well done. I am delighted that you did that so effectively. Is there anything you have learned from this that you would do differently next time?"

Play to your strengths - do what you are great at (keep honing these skills) and outsource or delegate what is not your core strength to the right person.

Knowing what to delegate is often challenging, as sometimes you might feel it's quicker or easier to do the task yourself. But you need to delegate tasks to develop your team as well as to ensure you are not doing everything.

To delegate, you first need to ensure that employees are clear regarding your expectations. Then you make them accountable for achieving this objective. Last, you monitor that they are on track and provide them with any support they may need.

When delegating, use clarifying questions to ensure the person is clear on what you have asked them to do, by when, and to what standards, etc.

Delegation enriches the jobs of employees and provides more challenges, authority and variety. It can also improve morale and employee motivation.

Task management meetings

I suggest you schedule a weekly task meeting with your employees to assess progress and review tasks etc. This ensures you are monitoring progress weekly with your employees and can offer support, assistance and coaching proactively as required. It also helps you to ensure staff are accountable and are achieving their tasks in line with their performance and role requirements.

At this meeting, your job is to ask employees to update you on progress, so use the following questions as a guide:

> **Do you want to take me through your tasks and update me on progress in relation to them?**
> **Do you need any additional support from me in relation to any of your tasks?**

> **Are you concerned in relation to any of them?**
>
> **I need you to do this project for me. Can you break down the tasks and come up with timelines to ensure this is done for x date?**
>
> **Have you more bandwidth to take on further tasks or responsibilities?**
>
> **Is there anything else you would like to discuss?**

Managing yourself

Do you spend time managing yourself? Do a self-assessment:

> **Am I getting enough good food to fuel my body and provide energy?**
>
> **Am I getting enough exercise?**
>
> **Am I getting enough fresh air?**
>
> **Am I getting to spend time with friends and family?**
>
> **Do I need to do a digital detox or to limit use of technology?**
>
> **Am I getting enough good sleep?**
>
> **Do I do positive affirmations about myself and my skills?**
>
> **Do I take time out to download what's going on in my head?**
>
> **Am I developing my knowledge and skills?**
>
> **Am I enjoying the journey?**

Schedule time in your diary to make sure you are doing what you enjoy and put an action plan in place for yourself to ensure you are enjoying the journey!

Top tips

- ❖ **Be clear on your role in managing the task, team and individual - are you doing the right things?**

- ❖ **Delegate effectively.**

- ❖ **Offer support.**

- ❖ **Encourage staff to self-reflect on learnings.**

- ❖ **Schedule a weekly task meeting to review progress with individuals on a one-to-one basis.**

- ❖ **Plan your time and schedule as much as possible at the start of the week.**

HIRING

Hiring is probably the most important job you do.

Great people are an organisation's most valuable resource and its key source of competitive advantage. The success of your team is also key to your personal and business success. So you need to ensure you recruit the best people to be part of your team. It's not hard to argue that **hiring is probably the most important job you do**. Without hiring the right people, your business cannot scale, grow or maximise its full potential and return on investment.

Making the wrong hiring decisions is not just a huge waste of time and resources; it's also a headache for the company and can negatively affect morale, revenue and customers. So it's worth spending time and money getting the recruitment process right from the start.

Do you need to hire someone?

This is the first question you should ask.

Take stock of the requirements of the business. Assess the gap you are trying to fill to decide whether you need to recruit someone. Will the work add value to the business? Is it necessary? Do you need an employee to do the job or can you outsource the task? Can the work be redeployed? Can it be automated?

Once you have made the business case that the role is required, ensure you are clear on what you are looking for.

Who are you looking for?

To decide who you need on the team, prepare a clear job and person specification. It's key that this new role adds value to the business through specific deliverables - so what are these outcomes the recruit needs to achieve? They should be really clear from the job specification.

When you are considering the selection criteria for the recruitment process, you also need to ensure you recruit candidates who are aligned to your cultural fit as well as having the core competencies to be able to do the job really well. For example, for me, a core value for every hire is **positivity** as it is so essential to team success and morale; just one negative person can spread negativity throughout your organisation.

How do you assess suitability?

Once you are clear on the criteria you are looking for, you need to decide the best tools to check which candidate is the best match. Your choices include interviews, presentations, occupational personality questionnaires, ability tests, etc.

Remember to focus on culture fit, competencies and outcomes throughout the selection process and assess each

candidate against these criteria. Each question you ask needs to be objective and applied consistently to all candidates to ensure you are legally compliant and fair to all candidates. To prove you have done this, you need to keep records – so bear this in mind from the outset. Otherwise, if a challenge is taken by an employee that they were discriminated against, you need to be able to prove that they were not selected on objective grounds. If the records are not complete, inferences may be drawn that may not help the company's case.

Screening candidates for interview is the next step. Use the essential criteria you have set for candidates to achieve. Record both the assessment criteria and scoring.

Again, at the interview, be clear on your criteria and match your questions to assess candidates against these criteria.

Ask open questions to see whether the candidate matches your requirements. For example, to check for the competence of customer focus, you might ask the candidate to give you an example of a time when they dealt with a very difficult customer and what they did in that situation. Open questions encourage candidates to express their views and can be used to elicit attitudes as well as facts.

It is essential that you get relevant information; listening is key to that. You can always ask follow-up questions if you need to clarify points or require further information. Your job is to 'peel the onion' and keep building on the information you have gleaned to assess the candidates' suitability.

Here are some sample interview questions:

What date did you do that?

What did that role involve?

Why did you leave?

What did you learn there?

What relationships did you foster there?

Why should we give you the job?

Where do you see yourself in five years?

Why are you applying for this job?

What has been your greatest achievement?

What excites you and lights you up at work?

What are the most important projects you worked on in that job?

How did you divide your time between your areas of responsibility?

Why do you wish to change your job / employer at this time?

How would your current employer react if you move on?

What do you consider to be your greatest strengths?

Have you worked with a group like this before? What was it like? How did you handle it?

Were you required to work alone as part of your previous job?

How would you define a positive work atmosphere?

Tell me about a time when, in difficult circumstances, you pulled the team together?

Tell me about a complex problem in your job and tell me how you dealt with them?

Give me an example of a very difficult decision for you that you made recently?

How do you organise and plan projects?

Describe a typical day in your job.

Tell me about a time when you came up with a new method / idea? How did you get it approved and implemented?

What was the most difficult situation you faced?

What have you done to become more effective in your position?

What interests you most about this position?

Why should I offer you this position?

So let's look at how you might structure these questions and choose the most suitable ones for a specific role.

INTRODUCTORY QUESTIONS

Did you have any problems finding us?

Can you tell us a little bit about yourself please?

What aspect of your job do you consider most crucial?

What would you say are the main qualities this job demands?

PREVIOUS EXPERIENCE QUESTIONS

What relevant experience do you have for this position?

Let's go through your CV in detail. Can you outline your role and responsibilities please?

How do you organise and plan projects in your current role?

What aspect of your current job do you most enjoy?

What aspect of your current job do you least enjoy?

What were your three most important responsibilities as part of your current job?

Why did you leave that role?

ADDITIONAL QUESTIONS

What achievements are you most proud of in relation to work?

How would your current employer react if you move on?

Why do you wish to change your job / employer at this time?

What kind of decisions are most difficult for you to make?

What are your training and development goals in line with skills or knowledge you would like to acquire?

Who inspires you and why?

If you owned this company, what would you suggest its top core values should be?

Can you teach me how to do something that I have no knowledge of before? Take me through the steps please.

Now YOU need to include some competency-focused questions based on the role requirements.

How do you assess competency?

Behavioural / competency interviews involve a series of structured questions designed to elicit information on specific behaviours. Questions are based on competencies directly linked to the requirements of the role.

Note that, for example, customer focus is a competence, while being genuine, inspiring and committed are behaviours.

Behavioural-based questions help the interviewer to evaluate candidates fairly and improve the match between people and jobs. The purpose of behavioural-based questions is to identify how a potential new employee would act in future situations. Research shows that the best predictor of future performance is past performance.

Competency questions assess what a person needs to do in order to carry out his / her job efficiently. Here are some examples of interview questions you might use to assess different competencies:

EMOTIONAL INTELLIGENCE

What do you consider to be your strengths relevant to this role?

What do you consider your areas for development?

What aspect of your work are you most passionate about?

Tell me about a time you faced conflict. How did you deal with it?

Describe something you find difficult about your role. How do you deal with this?

Who inspires you?

Why do they inspire you?

What do you consider to be the company's core values?

What are you most proud of in your career?

Describe a great relationship you have with a colleague?

Describe a time your received constructive feedback. How did you deal with it?

Who are the kind of people you would hire yourself?

Can you teach another person how to do xxxx? Talk me through the steps involved.

DRIVE AND DETERMINATION

What achievements are you most proud of to date?

Describe a situation that required a number of tasks to be done at the same time. How did you handle it?

What drives you to achieve your objectives?

BUILDING RELATIONSHIPS

What difficulties do you have in tolerating people with different backgrounds and interests from yours?

Describe a situation when you had to listen to a customer to understand their point of view.

Tell me about a time when you relied on a contact in your network to help you with a work-related task or problem.

Describe the type of person you get along with best. Why?

TAKING RISKS

Tell me about how you have worked with others to develop new and creative ideas to solve business problems?

How do you make your job easier or more rewarding?

Tell me about a time when you came up with a new method / idea. How did you go about trying to get it approved and implemented?

LEADERSHIP

Have you ever been in a situation in which you had to motivate others to take actions to support a major reorganisation? How did you do that?

Describe a time when you communicated a major new directive of senior management to employees. Which approaches worked and which did not?

PERFORMANCE MANAGEMENT

Tell me about a recent performance review you conducted with an employee. Describe what happened before, during, and after the review.

Tell me about a time when you worked with an employee to identify opportunities for their development. What process did you use?

INNOVATION AND CREATIVITY

Tell me about how you have worked with others to develop new and creative ideas to solve business problems.

Describe how you have improved the productivity / profitability of your work unit. How did you identify these opportunities for improvement?

Give me an example of a time when you were able to apply existing knowledge in a new way in order to solve a problem.

Tell me about a time when you came up with a new method / idea. How did you go about trying to get it approved and implemented?

Remember all these questions can be adapted for interviews when hiring people in leadership roles.

Interview tips

It's important to remember the following during interview:

❖ **Body language:** You can use positive body language to build a rapport with the candidate by having good eye contact, a firm handshake and a positive friendly tone of voice.

❖ **Active listening:** Be aware of blocks to active listening, including the lack of objectivity, empathy, concentration or patience.

❖ **Questioning techniques:** Each candidate should be asked the same set of questions to ensure that there will be no claim of treating candidates differently should a dispute about the interview process arise. But you can ask follow-up or probing questions, depending on how the initial question was answered.

Complementary assessment tools

I believe in **recruiting for attitude and training for aptitude** so, during recruitment, you need to assess whether the person's underlying personality characteristics will fit with your culture and core values in relation to the role they have applied for.

You can use occupational personality questionnaires to assess a candidate's fit with your required competencies and core values. These assessments are designed to provide businesses with information on an employee's behavioural style and how it is likely to impact their performance at work. These assessments are mainly used to find employees whose personalities align with the workplace culture and will be a good fit for the company, the team and the environment.

When choosing the most suitable personality test, make sure it is relevant to the job specification. Ensure it is developed with a clear understanding of the characteristics or personal traits you want to measure so that it gives your business clear results on the suitability of every candidate.

Consider at what stage of the recruitment process the test will be incorporated. You may decide to carry it out before or after second interviews, depending on the numbers of candidates at each stage of the recruitment project.

It is essential these assessments are administered by professionals who are trained to assess and interpret the results and that the tests are used in an appropriate professional and ethical manner. Tests should be designed by occupational psychologists and employers should ensure they source the test from a reliable source.

Reference checks

The main aim of a reference should be to confirm facts. Opinions given should be based on the facts known to the employer and, to avoid liability, employers giving references must take reasonable steps to ensure that any references given are accurate.

Always reference-check all potential candidates by telephone. Do a minimum of two reference checks.

So what do you need to find out? It is important to establish confirmation of employment details by asking the following questions:

In what capacity do you know the candidate and for how long?

Can you tell me the candidate's dates of employment, title, and role?

Can you confirm the responsibilities held by the candidate?

What do you think are the candidate's strong areas?

How would you describe the individual's overall performance?

What job do you think would be best suited to the individual's abilities?

In what areas do you think the candidate would need to develop?

What was his / her reason for leaving?

Did you have any issues with them during their employment?

Anything else you would like to tell me about them?

If your job was to depend on their success, would you recruit them?

Would you re-employ this person?

You can add to this list as you see appropriate.

In addition to these **fact-finding questions**, it is also important to probe based on the answers received in the interview and to explore the candidate's competencies further. Relevant questions, as suggested below, should be asked to back up this information or to probe further.

DRIVE AND DETERMINATION

Can you tell me about a time when he / she went that extra mile to get a client on board?

Tell me about how regularly he / she exceeded targets and what his / her highest achievement was?

AMBITION

What do you think his / her highest achievement was in his / her career or in his / her time in employment with you?

TAKING RISKS

Can you tell me about a time when he / she worked with others to solve a business problem?

> **LEADERSHIP**
>
> **Can you tell me about a time when he / she acted as an effective leader by motivating his / her team?**

Never overlook a warning signal – for example, a less than satisfactory reference. Consider an extra reference to probe further what has been highlighted as a concern.

Before you confirm a job offer, make sure satisfactory references, medical assessment, etc are in place. Ensure the candidate doesn't submit their notice to their current employer until then, just in case any concerns are highlighted during the process that means you won't be confirming the offer.

Also ensure that at all times all candidates are treated fairly and professionally. Remember they will talk about your company's professionalism or lack of it to other prospective candidates.

Now you have all the information based on all the selection criteria you have used, put it all together into a matrix to help you identify the most suitable candidate for the role. Hopefully you will now be in a position to recruit a superb candidate to join your team!

Top tips

* ❖ **Give hiring the right people the time and process it deserves – it is most important thing you do in business.**

* ❖ **Be clear on what you are looking for and remember you are selling the job to the candidate from the start of the recruitment process.**

* ❖ **Recruit for attitude, train for aptitude.**

* ❖ **Identify the best interview questions and assessment tools you need to use to source the best candidate.**

❖ Reference check at least two referees - always!

❖ Use complimentary tools to help make your recruitment decision easier - for example, occupational personality questionnaires.

❖ Keep clear and comprehensive records to show who you selected and why you selected them to confirm that your selection process was fair and transparent.

8 INDUCTION

The onboarding process starts once you meet the employee at recruitment.

Remember **the onboarding process starts once you meet the employee at recruitment**, as you started selling the job to them then. Now, at induction, you need to deliver on what you sold to the employee in terms of the company, culture, job, etc.

Induction

The aim of induction and onboarding is to establish rapport by accelerating new employees' settling in process, helping them to hit the ground running and giving them a sense of belonging.

At induction, outline the organisation's vision, mission, core values, current focus, future directions and provide an insight into the organisation's achievements. Introduce the organisational culture by explaining how things really work around here and the importance that is attached to issues such as punctuality, policies and procedures, work hours and codes of behaviour.

Clarify the job role and responsibilities by discussing the company's and department's expectations, and outlining how good performance will be assessed, measured and rewarded. Ensure the employee has a clear career path that shows their potential for growth and development, with clear goals and milestones from the start. Ask yourself:

> **Is there clear responsibility placed on someone to carry out the induction with new staff?**
>
> **Is the induction process structured to cover all the areas necessary?**
>
> **Does the person giving the induction take the opportunity to discuss the organisation's culture?**
>
> **Would a buddy and mentor system help to support the new employee?**
>
> **Is the employee engaged in the induction process and made to feel like an intrinsic part of the team?**
>
> **Is the employee met again a week or two afterwards and asked to assess the induction?**
>
> **How can we enhance our induction / onboarding?**

Employee feedback

During the onboarding process and at the end of it, obtain feedback on the effectiveness of the induction process from the new employee's perspective. This will help you to improve the experience for future hires.

It's important to ask the new employee these questions at the end of the induction process:

> **Have you been introduced to all the relevant people - your mentor, buddy, manager, colleagues in your department and relevant departments - you will be interacting with?**

Are you clear on our core values / mission / vision?

Do you fully understand your role and responsibilities?

Have you got clear SMART goals? Are you clear when we will review them?

Have you all the resources you need to do the job?

Can you use all systems and databases necessary for your role?

Have you had an opportunity to review all your employee documents? Do you have any questions? If not, let's get them signed off.

Is there information you need that has not been covered?

Have all policies and procedures relevant to your role been covered with you – for example, health and safety?

Has your mentor scheduled regular structured meetings with you in the next three months?

Is there anything else we can support you with?

Often companies wait for employees to ask questions and then they react, giving new employees only a quick introduction and hoping for the best. Up to 20% of staff turnover can occur in the first 45 days of employment, so your induction and onboarding needs to have a clear purpose, structure and plan. You need to measure its effectiveness and improve it based on constructive feedback from the most recent new hires.

Paperwork

Give the employee as much of the paperwork as you can in advance of their first day to give them the opportunity to review it, which avoids the need to spend most of the first day going through it. Instead use the induction as an opportunity to re-emphasise the importance of key aspects of the policies - for example, confidentiality - and give them an opportunity to ask any clarifying questions they may have.

Remember all employees in Ireland need to receive their contract of employment within two months of commencing their employment and their discipline and grievance procedure within 28 days of starting. Giving it to them in advance of their commencement and clarifying queries early is essential to a smooth integration so both parties are clear regarding what they are agreeing to and there is no ambiguity at a later stage.

In addition, an employee handbook provides this clarity in relation to policies and procedures.

Make sure everyone knows the new employee is starting, so they can prepare in advance for their arrival (email set up, etc.) and know their name when introduced to them.

If the employee is relocating from abroad or a different county / city, remember you may need to help them with the relocation process - to find new accommodation, schools for their children etc. There are companies that specifically assist with this process if you decide you want to outsource the process.

Manager, buddy or mentor?

Remember there is a difference between being the employee's **manager** (responsible for performance management / goal achievement, etc), their designated **buddy** (who will help them settle in and look out for them as their friend) and their **mentor** (an experienced professional who will act as their sounding board). Each has an important role in the employee's induction process so have you considered:

> **Who is the right person to be a buddy to this new employee?**
>
> **Who is the right person to mentor them?**
>
> **Is everyone clear on the role they are providing, including the employee?**

Remember, you want to avoid employees making the decision that this organisation is not for them due to the difficulty they have settling into their new role. This cost of turnover is a key issue for any organisation because revisiting the recruitment process is not only time-consuming, costly and a distraction for the business, it also means the job the new recruit was hired to do is not being done to the best benefit for the organisation.

Top tips

- ❖ **Ensure the induction is given the time it deserves.**
- ❖ **Ask the right questions to ensure the induction process is effective.**
- ❖ **Assign each new hire a buddy and mentor to help them settle into the organisation and new role.**
- ❖ **Ensure there is an on boarding pack prepared and given to the employee before or as soon as they start.**
- ❖ **Review the induction process to identify improvements to enhance it.**

9 COACHING

Feedback should always be specific
and future-focused.

Managing the performance of your employees proactively is really important to ensure your employees are clear on your expectations of them and that you support them in their role. So taking time out to discuss employee performance and to get their feedback on how they are performing is something you need to plan to do regularly during the employment relationship.

During probation

While an employee is on probation, it is essential that you meet the employee each month to assess their performance and to provide them with the support they need to help them settle into their new role.

If the employee is not performing to the required standard to match the job specification and role requirements, it is really important to have a constructive discussion with them as soon as possible so that the employee can address the issues and you can hear their feedback on any obstacles, issues, etc. they may be encountering. Often the employee may need training or retraining to resolve the problem.

However, if the employee is not improving after these performance meetings, you must remind them that, if they do not meet their required standard of performance after they have been given an opportunity to address your concerns, they could potentially fail their probation which will result in their employment being terminated. It is important that your feedback is really clear and specific so there is no ambiguity in relation to what you need improved.

Let's look at an example.

> Siobhan is a really nice person. She joined the company three months ago. She is still on probation but she hasn't been met yet formally to review her performance. You are not sure how she is doing overall in the role but you notice she seems stressed and is not meeting her weekly deadlines. You also are not receiving the reports and information that you need from her on time. Maybe it is just taking her longer to settle in than you had expected.
>
> **Scenario 1**
>
> You call Siobhan into your office and tell her you need to discuss her performance. You tell Siobhan that she doesn't seem to be getting along too well within the team atmosphere and that her deadlines are not being met on time each week. You remind Siobhan that her probation period is six months, which gives her three months to improve her performance and settle in with the company.

In contrast, scenario 2 shows how, by asking the right questions, you get the right information to help manage Siobhan's probation effectively.

Scenario 2

You ask Siobhan, "Is there a good time for us both to meet and have a chat about your first three months with the company?" Arrange a date and time and explain to Siobhan that you will be discussing how she feels she has settled into the company and her general performance so far. This gives Siobhan time to think about what she might like to bring up in the meeting and to review her own performance. You send her a follow-up memo to confirm this in advance of the meeting.

At the meeting, you start by saying, "Thank you, Siobhan, for attending this meeting. Although you are new to the company, you are a very valued employee. How do you feel the past three months within the company have gone for you?" You then listen carefully to what she says.

Siobhan says, "I am constantly stressed, as I'm not fully sure how to complete the reports and I'm too embarrassed to ask for help".

You explain to Siobhan that you had noticed that she seemed stressed at times and that the reports had been late. Remind Siobhan that you understand she is new to the job and you would never have expected her to pick up the reports on the first round. Ask Siobhan what she thinks could be done to help her get up to speed with the reports. Remind Siobhan that you and the company are there to support her in any way that you can. Agree on a SMART plan with Siobhan to tackle the issues raised in the meeting. Tell her that you are really pleased that you had the meeting and arrange to meet at another date.

You follow up with her by sending her a memo to confirm what you both discussed and agreed and to schedule the next meeting you will have with her.

Review meetings

After the employee has passed their probation, it is important that you still meet them regularly to assess their performance against the objectives you have jointly agreed.

A lot of the review forms that companies use can be very complex and daunting for both the employee and the manager to tackle. Sometimes, the forms can act as a deterrent for both parties to have the review meeting. **The most important part of the review meeting is asking the right questions and giving the employee the opportunity to be heard**. The form should act as an opportunity to prepare for the meeting by objectively assessing the performance in advance. It also acts as a guide for the meeting and as a record after the meeting to ensure everyone is clear on what has been agreed.

Using the last review goals that you agreed as a guide, you need to ask the following key questions at a performance review meeting:

> **What has been going well for you since our last meeting? For example, have you achieved the goals we agreed at the last meeting?**
>
> **What needs to be improved?**
>
> **What are the SMART goals we will agree going forward?**
>
> **Have you any other issues or concerns you would like to discuss?**

If you cover these key questions, then you will be proactively managing the employee's performance in line with their role requirements, holding them accountable to achieve their agreed goals, and you will be able to support the employee to maximise their performance.

Feedback

Giving employees on-going feedback and coaching is part of management – you need to try to do it at every chance you get, so you empower your team.

Feedback has four key objectives:

- ❖ To let people **know where they stand**.

- ❖ To provide a forum to **hear the employee's perspective**.

- ❖ To **reinforce and encourage** positive behaviour and performance.

- ❖ To **improve** behaviour and performance.

Coaching aims to ensure you are supporting the employee and developing them in their performance and in their career progression.

Always be sure you have all the facts before launching into feedback. It is always better to start by asking questions and listening – for example, it is better to ask, "Can you tell me about that customer complaint?" rather than giving out about how it was handled. Otherwise the employee will be defensive from the outset and it will be very difficult to agree an improved approach, which is the purpose of the meeting.

Great managers naturally find every opportunity to give feedback to their team and welcome it themselves as a continuous improvement process. Giving positive reinforcement and recognising great behaviour and great effort is essential to ensure employees accept that feedback is part of the company's core values and is an ingredient for continuous improvement. This also means that they will accept constructive feedback more positively when it is balanced, fair, objective and future-focused.

Giving feedback and coaching your team does not mean giving them all the answers. It means helping them think things through both positive situations and ones that need to be improved. By encouraging them to internalise the issue, you are ensuring there is a much higher chance that they will do it better next time or will emulate behaviours they know you appreciate.

It's sometimes easier to give people the solution as it saves you time as a manager and ensures the task will be done exactly as you want it, but as a good manager you need to empower and develop your team and by asking them the right questions to help them think through their options and help them find their own solutions, you will become a great coach.

Consider asking the following questions the next time an employee asks you for your help:

> **What do you see as the issue?**
> **Why?**
> **What do you think you should do?**
> **Are there any other options?**
> **What are the pros and cons for each option?**
> **What's stopping you?**
> **Have you any other concerns or issues?**
> **Is everything else OK with you?**
> **Can I do anything else to help or support you?**
> **So let's be clear, what is your SMART goal from this conversation?**
> **When will we follow up on progress? Let's agree a date and time now.**

Employee motivation is key to individual performance, group productivity and maintaining a pleasant work environment. Giving feedback and coaching employees is a key ingredient to staff morale.

Every behaviour has an underlying cause and taking the time to understand the cause of a behaviour and its motivating factors is key to changing or improving outcomes.

It is important that you create the right environment for the staff member in giving feedback and coaching them. **Remember always to praise in public and to give constructive feedback only in private.**

Always ensure the employee is clear on the purpose of the conversation - their own ongoing improvement.

Be specific with feedback

Feedback should always be specific and future-focused. You may have to look back on what has happened but it is important that you focus on what you need going forward. Remember you need to focus on the specific task or behaviour you need the employee to improve or achieve, so be crystal clear with them to ensure there is no ambiguity.

When giving employees feedback, the more specific you are in relation to the examples you use the clearer the employee will be on the improvement you are asking for. Outline the impact of their behaviours on the team and the overall business and explain the specific improvement required as a result.

Let's look at an example.

Oisin has been with the company for a number of years. He has recently made more errors than is acceptable and you are concerned that he is losing interest in the role as it is quite repetitive.

Scenario 1

You meet Oisin and you say, "Your current performance is not at the required standard. You need to improve".

He nods and says, "I will be more careful going forward".

You are concerned whether he really listened to you but you hope he did and that his performance will improve, as it is affecting customers.

Scenario 2

You meet Oisin and ask, "How are things going for you in your role?" He says, "I am getting bored as I've been here two years in the same job and it's very repetitive. But I like working with the company and the company culture and I like the team I work with".

You outline the requirement of the business regarding the standard of accuracy required and confirm also that you will keep an eye out for any internal opportunities for him as he is a valued employee. You ask, "Would you like to trial a different role on a Friday? I could do with some help with it – and it would add some variety to your role in the meantime". He is thrilled and says, "I'd love to do that". He commits to ensuring his accuracy and attention to detail will improve.

You record what you have discussed and agreed to ensure there is no ambiguity. For example, your follow-up email might read:

Dear Oisin

I would like to confirm what we agreed at our meeting today when we discussed your current performance. In particular I highlighted my concerns in relation to your recent high level of errors and outlined that a significant and consistent improvement is required.

You agreed to be more diligent and careful and we agreed to reassess the situation in the coming week and on a weekly basis for the coming two months. You confirmed that you are interested in a change of role if any other opportunities come up as you feel you would like a change as you are in this role for two years now and it is very repetitive. I confirmed that I would let you know about any internal opportunities and confirmed that we will trial you in the QSR department on a Friday to see how that goes as we need extra help there currently.

If I can do anything else to support you, just let me know as you are a valued member of the team. However, the business requires all staff members' performance to be at the required level to ensure you meet your role requirements and the customers' expectations. I

appreciate your assurances that your current level of
accuracy will improve in this regard.

Remember that any performance meeting is also an opportunity to motivate your team, so ensure you check in regularly to confirm they are OK and to offer your support to help them in any way you can.

Outlining the company's core values at induction (see **Chapter 8**) means that performance discussions with staff who are displaying behaviour in conflict with the values are much more focused. For example, if you have an employee who is not being a team player, you can go back to the core values to explain that it is an essential requirement for all employees who work in the organisation to live the company's core values as these values set the standard for all employees.

Let's look at an example.

Ross seems to be very negative. "That's just the way he is, there is no point talking to him", or so everyone says.

Scenario 1

You meet Ross and tell him, "You need to be less negative. Your negative attitude is affecting the whole team. I'm very unhappy about it. If your attitude doesn't improve immediately, it may result in disciplinary action".

Scenario 2

You focus on asking Ross the right questions to elicit agreement to display the company core values going forward.

You ask Ross whether he is aware of the company's core values. Ross says, "I'm not sure". You outline them for him: positivity, integrity and customer focus. You then ask him whether he displays these behaviours proactively in all his interactions with his team, customers and suppliers. He says, "I'm not sure".

You outline that you are concerned that he doesn't display them in line with the company's core values and that he needs to reassess his approach as these are the behaviours all staff need to display consistently. This is a really fundamental requirement of working in this company and is a core part of his performance requirements. You agree to meet him on a bi-weekly basis to assess how he is proactively displaying these behaviours and at each meeting you will need him to give you examples of how he has done this. You will also be monitoring his interactions.

At the next meeting with Ross, focus on the examples he offers in relation to these core values. If he has failed to improve or to proactively display these skills, you will need to be very specific in relation to asking him why. You need to get to the root of the problem now that he is aware of the company's requirements.

If people do not hear, absorb and engage with you when you are giving feedback or coaching, it is unlikely they will take your feedback on board. So you must **ensure that you are having**

this conversation at the right time, in the right environment and in the right context.

Focus on outcomes

It is also important to remember we have all different work styles and no one approach is best. If an employee prefers a different approach and it achieves the same goal, you need to respect their approach rather than expecting a universal work-style as that is not realistic. So **focus on outcomes.** Asking them the right questions rather than giving them your advice will help them to achieve the approach that best suits their style of work and personality and will still achieve the right outcome.

Many managers give feedback by "managing by wandering around", a phrase coined by Tom Peters, who encouraged managers to be curious and helpful in supporting their employees. By wandering around you are integrating coaching and feedback into your daily management of your team.

Follow-up

Feedback and coaching is an on-going and continuous process. This means you need to set in place a regular follow-up process to ensure that the employee feels supported and knows that they are accountable for achieving what you have agreed.

I find that, **if you don't diary the follow-up at the time of the first meeting, it is unlikely the follow-up meeting will happen** unless there is a performance management or disciplinary crisis. Then it's too late to nip things in the bud, so tackle any concerns early – follow-up is key to this proactive approach.

So remember to give performance management and feedback lots of time in your schedule because the benefits of on-going regular feedback cannot be overestimated in terms of the benefit it gives to the organisation.

Top tips

- ❖ **Staff want feedback – more than you think; both constructive and positive feedback so give them double the amount you think they need.**

- ❖ **Coach and ask – do not tell.**

- ❖ **Give feedback and performance management lots of time in your management schedule and try to manage by walking around as well as by having formal performance meetings.**

- ❖ **Be honest and clear.**

- ❖ **Record your SMART goals and what you have agreed.**

- ❖ **Set the date and time for the next review meeting before the current one ends.**

10 GRIEVANCES

You are obliged to follow your company's
grievance procedure consistently.

All companies are obliged to have a disciplinary and grievance procedure in place for all their employees and to give them a copy within 28 days of their employment start-date.

When employees flag that they have a grievance, the grievance procedure is the first step you need to refer to because **you are obliged to follow your company's grievance procedure consistently**.

If an employee raises an issue, you need to give them the opportunity to be heard and to identify what they want you to do to resolve the issue. It's important that you remember your job as their manager is to signpost them and to outline the options available to them. Ideally, you will try to see whether you can nip the issue in the bud but you must also outline the options in the grievance procedure, including the informal and formal routes.

If employees have grievances regarding their working conditions or requests, ensure you ask them to put them in writing for you to ensure you are clear about the issue and have a paper trail.

The grievance process

The **informal route** generally involves encouraging the employee to address the issue themselves initially (perhaps by talking to the other employee they have the grievance with) if they are happy to do this or to use mediation.

Mediation is usually included in most companies' informal grievance process because it is particularly effective in helping to resolve interpersonal conflict between two fellow workers or an employee and their supervisor / manager.

Employees can skip the informal process and move to the next stage if they feel the informal approach will not address the issue.

The **formal process** involves the employee making a formal statement and outlining their complaint. This complaint is then investigated fairly and comprehensively, following which the investigator will recommend appropriate action - perhaps even disciplinary action (see **Chapter 11**).

The most important thing in dealing with grievances is to ensure that you address the issue presented. No matter what the issue, remember that **if the employee considers it a grievance, it needs to be addressed and treated professionally** in line with the company's grievance policy. The employee always owns the grievance and it is up to them how they proceed with it in line with your policy, unless they highlight something of such significance that you are compelled to address the issue immediately - for example, child or elder abuse.

Let's look at some examples.

Danny and Maurice are not getting on; you think it might be something to do with a staff night out but you aren't sure. You haven't done anything yet in the hope that the issue will settle itself. However, Maurice has come to you today to tell you he wants to make a complaint about Danny but he doesn't want you to tell Danny.

Scenario 1

You listen to Maurice and empathise with him. He tells you, "Danny is blanking me. I don't know why - and I'm annoyed about it".

You thank Maurice for letting you know and you tell him to come back to you if anything more serious happens.

What do you think? Will this approach resolve or improve the issue for either of the employees or for the business?

No, it definitely will not. And you could also have given Maurice the impression that you are on his side, which as a manager you cannot be at any stage - you must remain objective. He might also think that, because you know about his concerns, you might do something "behind the scenes". However, this is outside the scope of your role as a manager and things could go pear-shaped very quickly if you were to take this approach.

So let's look at scenario 2 which is a better approach to the same problem: by asking the right questions and listening, you can solve this grievance proactively.

Scenario 2

You thank Maurice for coming to you and confirm that you are going to refer to the employee grievance procedure from his staff handbook. You confirm that complaints or grievances cannot be anonymous; if the employee wants you to do something about a concern, it needs to be in line with the grievance procedure. You ask Maurice whether he is familiar with the procedure and go through it with him. You explain that your role in the process is to signpost him and to remain objective as you have only heard one side of the story so far. However, you will support him to decide on the best next step in any way you can.

You ask Maurice to confirm how he would like you to proceed with his issue. You suggest he consider the informal route initially, but he says he doesn't feel comfortable going to Danny himself.

You then discuss the option of mediation. You explain what is involved and that it would be facilitated by an experienced and trained mediator who is completely objective. You explain that Danny would have to be agreeable to this process also.

You also explain to Maurice that he has the option of making a formal complaint and that it has to be his decision on how he would like to progress. You explain he can take some time to decide and that you are available to answer any questions he may have in relation to the options.

He takes this time and returns the following day to confirm he would like to progress with mediation. You get the wheels in motion to do this, as outlined in the grievance procedure.

Natural justice

All parties are entitled to fair procedures and the principles of natural justice. These include:

❖ That employee grievances are fairly examined and processed.

❖ That details of any allegations or complaints are put to the employee concerned.

❖ That the employee concerned is given the opportunity to respond fully to any such allegations or complaints.

❖ That the employee concerned is given the opportunity to avail of the right to be represented during the procedure.

❖ That the employee concerned has the right to a fair and impartial determination of the issues concerned, taking into account all appropriate evidence, factors and circumstances.

Investigations

When investigating grievances, ask these key questions during your fact-finding:

What is the behaviour / issue at the core of the grievance?

When did the behaviour / issue occur? Seek specific dates, if possible.

Who was responsible for the behaviour / issue? What did they do? What did they say?

Were there any witnesses? Who were they?

Did the employee raise a grievance at any stage to management?

What does the employee see as an ideal solution to their grievance?

How do they want to progress their grievance?

Your job is to get someone to investigate the employee grievance thoroughly, objectively and fairly. You may do this yourself or it might be better to get someone else to do it for you.

This investigation is designed to find the facts and to elicit the details of the employee's grievance. It often means having to **probe to get under the iceberg to get to the real problem** – what has caused the employee to raise this grievance. Employees' behaviour masks their perceptions, attitudes, values and beliefs – all powerful emotional drivers that are hidden below the waterline.

Remember that, as well as both parties, witnesses should also be met and the investigator needs to ask them probing questions too to ensure they get the full facts.

Resolving grievances

Some grievances cannot be resolved to the employee's desired solution – for example, an employee requests parental leave to allow them be on a three-day week but the company can't facilitate this in line with business requirements or an employee may be aggrieved because they want enhanced terms and conditions but the company cannot meet their expectations.

Remember that dealing with your employees consistently and fairly is important to ensure you don't set a precedent that causes issues with another employee or doesn't meet the business requirements at a later date.

Ask lots of probing questions to see whether there are any solutions to their grievance you can help address.

Give the employee any options you can offer them. Allow them time to consider them. Put the options to them in writing.

Being honest, following the process, asking the right questions, listening to the answer, and being fair to all employees by treating them consistently are the key elements in managing employee grievances proactively.

Top tips

- ❖ **Nip issues in the bud – proactively address issues if they exist.**

- ❖ **Refer to the company grievance policy and procedure and ensure you follow it consistently.**

- ❖ **Know your role in the process – you must be objective, signpost the employee and follow the grievance procedure and process.**

❖ **The employee owns the grievance and you must let them decide what they want to do - you just need to give them the options.**

❖ **Ensure grievances are dealt with fairly and in line with the rules of natural justice and the company's policy.**

❖ **Sometimes you can't address the grievance to the employee's required level of satisfaction or solution - be honest and consistent and explain why that is the case.**

11 DISCIPLINARY

The main purpose of the disciplinary
process is improvement.

The aim of the disciplinary procedure is to address the issue and to ensure that the performance or behaviour of the employee improves. On occasion, however, it requires the issuing of a warning or ultimately, in serious situations or in repeated incidents of breaching the company policy, termination of the employee's contract of employment.

The disciplinary process

So let's consider the best approach to handle a disciplinary situation in line with your legal obligations.

You may need to invoke the disciplinary procedure if an employee's performance is not at the required standard and you have done everything you could to support them to improve or if an employee breaches policy or procedures. **Ensuring you follow the company's disciplinary procedure is essential** in both situations. Any sanction must be reasonable and proportionate.

The underlying principles of dealing with disciplinary matters includes giving the employee:

- ❖ A fair and impartial hearing.
- ❖ The right to representation.
- ❖ A chance to be heard.
- ❖ The opportunity to appeal any decision that is made.

There needs to be a separation of process during disciplinary proceedings. There are three separate strands:

- ❖ The investigation held and completed by the investigation manager.
- ❖ The outcome held and completed by the outcome manager.

❖ The appeal held and completed by the appeal manager.

The purpose of the investigation is to get the full facts and evidence in relation to the allegation at issue. This must be done impartially and completely. It is also important to meet witnesses if they are named, to ensure you do a comprehensive investigation and to give the employee the opportunity to give their feedback in relation to the investigation, so they get a full opportunity to be heard. Remember that everyone is innocent in the process until a sanction is issued. Being objective and treating all parties involved with dignity, respect and confidentiality helps to ensure these matters are dealt with professionally.

There is no such thing as a summary dismissal; you always need to follow the process!

So let's look at some examples.

Julia has been persistently late in the last month. You have mentioned it to her many times informally and have told her that, if it happens again, it will result in disciplinary action. She is late again this week, so you feel you need to meet her to progress the matter to disciplinary action at this stage.

Scenario 1

You ask Julia to come to a disciplinary meeting the next day to discuss her on-going lateness. She resigns when she gets the letter. You are not sure what you should do now: accept her notice or continue with the disciplinary meeting to understand what is going on?

Scenario 2

You ask Julia to meet you but you do not tell her it is a disciplinary meeting as you have not yet met her formally regarding her lateness. You are concerned that this behaviour is not usual for her so you feel you need to have an initial 'drawing the line in the sand' meeting to explain that the lateness is causing operational issues and to understand what is going on in her life.

When you meet Julia, you ask, "Is everything OK for you? It's not the norm for you to be late. You are a valued employee with the company so I want to see if I can support you". You feel she is upset and you give her a minute. She then says, "I am having a really difficult time with childcare just now".

You agree with Julia that you need to come with a plan to help resolve this issue with her as you cannot accept her being late going forward on an on-going basis as the business requirements mean she must be on time to meet the customers' needs. She appreciates the dilemma that this presents, understands the matter needs to be resolved and appreciates the opportunity to address it.

Sometimes you need to meet the employee and give them a chance prior to engaging with the disciplinary procedure.

Remember being firm but fair is important when managing people and asking them "Is everything OK?" is crucial!

Remember that the main purpose of the disciplinary process is improvement.

Let's look at a second example.

> You find out that Mario, your IT developer, is spending lots of time every day on the Internet on non-work-related matters. He is a really good employee and his skillset is hard to find. You are disappointed in him. You decide to meet him to discuss this very serious breach of procedure.
>
> **Scenario 1**
>
> You bring Mario into your office and ask him to explain his behaviour as you know he has breached the IT procedure. You explain that this is not acceptable and that he will be going down the road of disciplinary action if this occurs again. You hope he

has listened and understands how inappropriate his behaviour has been.

Scenario 2

You send Mario a memo inviting him to a disciplinary meeting, saying that it has been brought to your attention that he has allegedly breached the company's IT policy by spending time during work on the Internet doing personal tasks.

When Mario comes to your office for the meeting you confirm he knows why he is here and ask him what he has to say for himself. He says he only does it because he works extra hours for which he is not paid and feels that, as a result, he can spend some of his work time on the Internet to make up the balance. He says he is really sorry that he totally took advantage of the fact he is given lots of autonomy at work and apologises sincerely. You feel that he is genuine and you highlight that, even though you are really disappointed in him, you feel that you can draw a line in the sand once you have his commitment that this won't happen again. He confirms that there is no chance he will do anything to jeopardise his role again and that he had no excuse for his behaviour. He says he appreciates the fact that he was given the opportunity for a second chance.

In scenario 2, by asking rather than just telling Mario, you have got an understanding into why he behaved the way he did even though it's unacceptable. You also got him to commit to ensuring the behaviour won't happen again - and you believe it won't.

Let's look at a third example.

Robert has taken €100 from the till. You saw him put the money in his pocket. You are shocked and devastated; you trusted him in his role. You want to fire him immediately.

Scenario 1

You call Robert into your office and you ask him what he has done. He shrugs and asks, "What you are talking about?" You tell him what you saw. He denies what he did and says you must have made a mistake. You have no idea what you are going to do now!

Scenario 2

You take some time to review the till balance that evening to see whether it has balanced and you also look at the CCTV to confirm what you saw. Based on all the evidence, you are concerned that Robert has taken the money.

You therefore feel you are not the best person to do an investigation in and so you ask someone else to do it for you to ensure the process stands up and the right outcome is achieved.

You feel you are not the best person to do an investigation as you have witnessed the event and you have an emotional bias against Robert now. You want to ensure everything is done correctly. To ensure there is separation of process, you ask another management member to investigate the incident. This way, the process will stand up and the right outcome will be achieved.

If you feel out of your depth dealing with a disciplinary process, then it's important that you 'press pause' and get professional advice. **Remember nothing must be dealt with immediately but everything must be dealt with correctly** by following the process fully when dealing with your team - in particular, in complex areas like the disciplinary process.

Top tips

- ❖ **Be proactive dealing with disciplinary issues - the longer they fester, the bigger the problem.**
- ❖ **Follow the disciplinary process exactly and consistently.**
- ❖ **The paper trail must be maintained at each step of the process.**

❖ **If you can't be objective, get a colleague to handle the process for you.**

❖ **Every disciplinary sanction has an appeal option.**

❖ **Nothing must be dealt with immediately but everything must be dealt with correctly.**

❖ **If in doubt, get professional advice.**

12 TALENT

Consider how you can harness and maximise the potential of your team.

Talent management is essential to retain the right people to give you an edge over your competitors.

How can you harness talent in your organisation?

Most organisations still retain employees by improving reward-related packages - they pay higher wages. But more is required to retain employees now.

Employees today want to know they are part of a bigger picture and are contributing to the overall goals; they want clear objectives; they want work-life balance; they want to be empowered.

As a people manager, you need to consider how you can harness and maximise the potential of your team. To me, there are two key aspects to talent management:

- ❖ Performance management - covered earlier in this book.
- ❖ Training and development.

These aspects of talent management are complemented by all the other areas of people management included in this book.

Have you a succession plan in place?

A succession plan means that you have a strategy for developing potential future leaders and that the staff are aware of the opportunities for growth and development within your organisation. This is an excellent motivational tool, as employees can see career progression opportunities as the organisation grows and new roles are created or when an employee leaves.

So consider these questions:

> **Who is the number 2 for key roles in the organisation and in my department?**
>
> **Who is my number 2?**
>
> **What are the training gaps based on current knowledge and skills?**

Training and development

Managers must strive for a performance-driven environment. This involves having an understanding of each employee's skills, capabilities and behaviours. **People are like electricity - of little use unless they are switched on!**

As a manager, you need to figure out how people develop over time and what kind of behaviours lead to success - how people build confidence with stakeholders, for example, by providing an excellent service. You need to work collaboratively with your employees to agree their individual training and development plans. You must also consider future organisational needs when identifying performance or learning / knowledge gaps.

You must nurture and develop talent as this focus on employee development will ensure that the organisation is seen as an attractive place to work.

Identifying training gaps and needs

A training needs analysis will help you establish the training gaps in your team.

Consider for each employee their current role, performance and areas of interest. Consider what they must achieve to develop themselves and to drive the business forward.

Once you have established this, you must decide whether the employee has the skills and knowledge to develop in this way. Identify the training needed to develop the employee and consider where the employee should be placed in your organisation once they have acquired these skills and knowledge.

When doing a training needs analysis, ask:

What are the key goals of the organisation?

What are the current skills in each department?

What skills and knowledge is required in each department to meet the business objectives?

What training work experience should our employees be undertaking?

Once the plans have been developed and the training undertaken, how will we measure that the training needs have been accomplished?

> **What are the future skills gaps, trends and opportunities we need to be developing now - for example, based on technology changes, etc?**
>
> **Based on succession plan requirements, is there a training requirement?**

What is the best approach to this training need?

Next, you need to research the training opportunities available for your team and decide the best approach. Ask:

> **Who will conduct the training?**
>
> **Will the training be in-house or external?**
>
> **What will it cost?**
>
> **What time will be involved?**
>
> **What exactly will the employee achieve during this training?**
>
> **Will the training objectives and needs of the business be fully met or will further training be required?**
>
> **Training involves courses, e-learning and blended learning - what is the best approach?**

How can you maximise the benefit of training?

Now that a team member has received training, you need to maximise the benefits for your department and for the organisation. This is often where good time and money is lost as employees return to work but the training opportunity is not maximised.

Training transfer starts before the employee attends the training session by identifying with them the key learnings they will gain and how these will be beneficial to the department and organisation. This ensures they are focused on transfer from the get-go.

Ask the employee:

> **What is the benefit of this training for you?**
>
> **What is the benefit of this training for the department and the company?**
>
> **What are the key skills / knowledge / attitudinal learnings you need to gain from the training?**
>
> **What will success from this training look like?**

After the employee comes back from completing the training, you need to evaluate whether they are applying the training. It's important to conduct a post-training session with each trainee a couple of weeks after the training. In this session with the employee, ask:

How have you applied learned skills since attending the training?

What outcomes have you / can you put into action?

How do you think you can apply what you have learned from this practice to future development in the department / company?

Are there any areas you would recommend we improve / change based on your learning?

Are there any skills / knowledge learned from the training programme that you have yet to apply?

What are your plans / timeframes to put these skills into action?

What support do you need from me (as your manager) or your team?

Ongoing development of your staff is critical. **It's not enough to hire the best people; you've got to keep the best people too!** This is often challenging but I love Richard Branson's comment: "Train people well enough so they can leave, but treat them well enough that they don't want to". If you stick to that, you won't go far wrong.

Top tips

❖ **Talent management involves many aspects but particularly performance management and training and development.**

❖ **Identify training gaps based on employee performance gaps and future organisational needs.**

❖ **Decide on the type of training that is best to facilitate the training and learning required.**

❖ **Focus on maximising learning and training transfer by having a pre- and post-training meeting.**

13 TRUST

**Engage with your team and ask
what's important for them.**

There are many aspects to fostering employee trust, morale and satisfaction. In this chapter, I have taken the top tips from our learnings working with diverse organisations.

When we do employee surveys or focus groups for clients, lack of communication and feedback are at the top of the list of what employees would like their employer to improve - even in organisations that have a lot of communication.

Enhance your communication with your team

Consider enhancing your current level of employee communications to increase staff involvement.

Ask yourself:

> **Am I holding enough staff meetings where staff may communicate with their team members?**
>
> **Are there sufficient options for open communication?**
>
> **Are effective systems of two-way (written, face-to-face and by telephone) communication encouraged?**
>
> **Am I doing enough one-to-one meetings with my employees?**
>
> **Do I need to introduce an employee survey once a year so I really get to know what my team are thinking and what they need?**

The responsibility for effective communication with staff lies with managers and depends on the cooperation of all staff – but you need to emphasise how important it is to you. You also need to encourage your open door policy to be a reality in your management style by giving employees time and actively listening.

Encourage your team to give their opinion where their experience allows and educate staff in the skills and benefits of communication. Encourage them also to engage in blue sky thinking and in offering proactive solutions.

Highly-motivated employees are essential if your company is to maximise future growth. Such motivation is primarily a function of employees having both knowledge and discretion within their areas of operation. **A clear, understandable and achievable plan is key to cascading and communicating tasks and responsibilities to all members of staff.**

Advocate honesty

Be honest – that's the only way you can foster real trust. Set a good example by being honest yourself and working to high moral and ethical standards.

Refer to honesty in the employee's induction and in the company's mission statement. Introduce an honesty policy in which honesty is encouraged and respected. This will help to protect the employee, the employer and customers from any dishonest acts by other employees, customers, suppliers or the general public. Identify the expectations employees are expected to meet and what they should do if they feel that the policy has been breached by another stakeholder, including the employer. It is important that the policy is explicit on how an employee can report wrongdoing – privately or anonymously if they wish – without fear of recriminations or victimisation as a consequence of their honesty.

Develop trust

Trust is key to a successful business – but can easily be damaged.

Recent years have seen frequent cutbacks and redundancies, which can create an atmosphere of mistrust in an organisation and have a negative impact on morale so it is important for employers to reassure the employees that remain and to focus on employment involvement and development.

Be consistent

Be consistent in the way that you manage people. It is not ideal for employees to come to work not knowing what mood the boss may be in today. Bad moods can be infectious – use your emotional intelligence to regulate your emotions and to maintain a stable work environment.

Be open

Even when things may not be going so smoothly, it's important that staff are not left in the dark. If a mistake is made, face it openly, take responsibility and work together towards finding a solution.

Development and career paths

Whereas in the past money was considered the main driver for retaining employees, nowadays employees are looking for more. Today's employee wants to feel part of a bigger picture and to be valued by the company they work for. They also want to be given an opportunity to develop within the business and to increase their knowledge and skills.

Employee engagement

When employees are not positively engaged, job satisfaction and productivity will be negatively affected. In organisations where employee engagement is evident, it can have an incredibly beneficial impact as staff feel valued and happy in their roles.

When analysing the effectiveness of employee engagement in your organisation, ask:

Do staff have the knowledge and resources they need to do their jobs?

Have managers outlined the company mission, values and vision?

What are the employees' goals and fears?

What direction do the employees see the business going in and how do they see the business getting there?

Are employees being rewarded for accomplishing goals? Is the reward meaningful to each employee?

Is an annual appraisal carried out with all staff and a training plan established with each employee?

Work-life balance

It's important to endeavour to establish an equilibrium for both ourselves and our employees. A good work-life balance includes working a standard time each day from approximately five to nine hours, having interests outside of work and taking sufficient rest and meal breaks during the day.

Management should aim to provide employees with their roster as far in advance as possible so employees can make plans for their after-work activities. Supporting flexibility in the workplace can also improve productivity and morale.

Employers must also keep in mind the legislation that governs working arrangements and which protects workers' rights to rest and leave entitlements. Examples of this legislation include:

- ❖ **The Organisation of Working Time Act, 1997**, which outlines rest entitlements

- ❖ **Maternity Protection Acts, 1994 and 2004 / Parental Leave Acts, 1998 and 2006**, which outlines a parent's entitlement to time off to care for a new-born / newly-adopted child.

- ❖ **Carer's Leave Act, 2001**, which sets out the entitlement to time off to care for a dependent

In addition, employees have the right to *force majeure* leave, which allows them leave work in the case of an emergency.

Encourage employees to manage their work-life balance and to be off when they are off so they will be recharged and renewed when they come back to work to maximise their productivity.

Absenteeism and presenteeism

Absence occurs during the life cycle of the employee for a variety of reasons. Back pain, injury and stress are the most commonly-cited problems on medical certificates for medical absence.

It is essential that employers ensure that they are fulfilling their duty of care to their employees by including manual handling and work-related stress when conducting risk assessments as part of their review of the company's Health & Safety Statement.

Ask:

> **Could some of these illnesses have been prevented?**
>
> **Does my organisation have an effective control programme and ergonomic design of work tasks?**
>
> **Are staff trained correctly in regard to lifting techniques – for example, manual handling training (which all employers are recommended to get staff to complete)?**
>
> **Do we have a clear and comprehensive absence / sick leave policy?**

Your absence / sick leave policy should cover these key areas:

- ❖ Notification procedures.

- ❖ Certification procedures.

- ❖ Sick leave payment (if any).

❖ Referral to company doctor procedures.

❖ Return to work procedures.

❖ Support process for the absent employee.

The consequences of a failure to follow the absence / sick leave policy must be clearly outlined. All staff should be fully aware of the policy: each member of staff should be issued with the policy in writing and they should be asked to sign to confirm that they have read and understood it.

It is vital that management implement the policy within the organisation in every case. All staff should be treated equally under the policy in order to prevent any claims of unfair treatment or discrimination arising.

It is important to foster an attendance culture within your organisation and ensure that you tackle both short- and long-term absenteeism.

Short-term absenteeism can cause the most disruption to employers in terms of sourcing last-minute cover for the employee. Therefore, it is important for line managers to conduct return-to-work meetings with employees who have short-term absenteeism to ascertain the reasons for the illness, whether the employee is fit to return to work and the likelihood of the illness reoccurring.

At this meeting, ask the employee:

What was the illness / reason for absence?

Was the illness work-related?

Are you feeling 100% better?

Is there a reason for a pattern (if any) of short-term absence?

Is there anything you need on your return to work?

Do you think there may be a reoccurrence of the illness?

Keep open channels of communication and update the employee on what they have missed since they were out.

Line managers must monitor absenteeism and, if a pattern emerges for one employee or if there is a high incidence of absenteeism, the issue may become a disciplinary matter.

Where an employee has gone on **long-term absenteeism**, it is important for an employer to maintain contact with the employee to understand whether it is likely that they will return to work in the future. An employee on long-term absenteeism should continue to submit sickness certificates and keep the employer updated on their likely return-to-work date.

An employer should have a policy that allows referral of an employee to a company-appointed doctor to assess independently when the employee can return to work or whether the employee will require alternative employment in the organisation.

Overall, managing absenteeism is a tricky area for an employer to navigate. Nonetheless, given the associated costs and the requirement to support your employee at a potentially difficult time for them, it is important for employers to be proactive in **managing absenteeism**.

Presenteeism is becoming more prevalent in workplaces. It refers to productivity loss resulting from staff with health problems continuing to attend work despite illness, injury or distress.

Due to its silent nature, presenteeism can be both harder to monitor and to address than absenteeism. It's not always obvious that someone has mentally checked out until performance and productivity suffer significantly.

Wellbeing of employees at work

Key to creating a wellbeing-focused work environment are knowledge and awareness. **Introducing methods that protect employees' wellbeing can help prevent a number of illnesses**, which in turn can help reduce absenteeism and presenteeism.

As an employer you can work to ensure wellbeing in the workplace by:

❖ Providing **training** on topics to help reduce stress or to create awareness – for example, time management, assertiveness, company culture awareness, wellbeing and mental health awareness, dignity and respect.

❖ Providing **information** on wellness ideas – for example, fitness classes, nutritional ideas.

❖ Creating **an open environment** for employees to learn about their own wellbeing and to share ideas with their colleagues.

❖ Developing **ideas** for improving happiness and well-being at work – for example, have brainstorming sessions with your team about what you could do that would help improve the culture of the company.

❖ **Meeting with employees** one-to-one on a regular basis to discuss performance and goals.

❖ Identifying and assessing how material conditions, work, productivity, income levels and stability, etc interact with employee's personal resources – for example, autonomy, competence, feeling safe and secure, connected with others – to **create happiness at work**. Do this for every employee.

The **benefits of ensuring wellbeing in the workplace** are:

❖ Enhanced recruitment and retention of healthy employees.

❖ Decreased rates of illness and injuries.

❖ Reduced employee absenteeism.

❖ Improved employee relations, morale and satisfaction.

❖ Increased productivity.

Taking preventative initiatives regarding health and wellbeing are now common to enhance employee wellbeing at work.

Many organisations use an employee assistance programme (EAP) to complement the internal supports offered to employees.

EAPs provide employees, and sometimes their families, with confidential services to deal with personal issues from health to financial matters. When an employee avails of the programme, they receive assistance with identifying and resolving personal concerns such as stress, marital, financial, health, dependency or other personal issues.

Details of the company EAP should be contained in the employee handbook as well as on the staff notice board. Employees should be informed of how to contact the EAP service during their induction. Management may refer employees to the EAP at any time if they deem it prudent to do so but, in such cases, they must be careful not to attempt analysis or judgement of the employee's problem.

EAP services are highly confidential and management does not receive feedback unless the employee gives written consent.

Fostering a culture of dignity and respect

As a manager, you have a duty of care to protect your employees' health and safety at work, including preventing the risk of bullying and harassment at work.

Bullying and harassment can have a major negative effect in an organisation. **Encourage a workplace free of bullying and harassment through regular training and having a Dignity and Respect at Work policy.**

The Workplace Relations Commission's Code of Practice on addressing **bullying** in the workplace defines bullying as:

Repeated inappropriate behaviour, direct or indirect, whether verbal, physical or otherwise, conducted by one or more persons against another or others, at the place of work and / or in the course of employment, which could reasonably be regarded as undermining the individual's right to dignity at work. An isolated incident of the behaviour described in this definition may be an affront to dignity at work but, as a once off incident, is not considered to be bullying.

Bullying may involve single or repeated incidents, ranging from extreme forms of intimidating behaviour, such as physical violence, to more subtle forms such as ignoring someone. It can often occur without witnesses.

Harassment is defined as:

Any act of conduct which is unwelcome and offensive, humiliating or intimidating on a discriminatory ground including spoken words, gestures, or the production, display or circulation of written material or pictures.

Sexual harassment is defined as:

Any form of unwanted verbal, non-verbal or physical conduct of a sexual nature which has the purpose or effect of violating a person's dignity and creating an intimidating, hostile, degrading, humiliating or offensive environment for the person.

It is often preferable for all concerned that complaints of bullying or harassment are dealt with informally whenever possible, as an informal approach can often resolve matters. The objective should be to resolve the difficulty quickly and effectively, with the minimum of conflict and stress for the individuals. Your job is to monitor issues that may be bubbling under the surface and nip issues in the bud and so foster a real culture of dignity and respect as a core value within your team.

If issues do occur, as with the grievance procedure outlined earlier in this book, you must refer to your bullying policy and, ensure that your company procedure is followed. This procedure must be open and transparent and in line with the rules of natural justice. Confidentiality is also a key factor.

Social connections and fun at work

Encourage employees to have a social connection at work and to make work as much fun as possible. This might be fostered *via* team initiatives or social events around the area of wellbeing or charitable initiatives.

Rather than organising what you think the team would enjoy, leave it to them to organise what they would like to do - this helps build initiative within your team.

The best approach, though, is to engage with your team and ask them what's important for them so you can tailor the initiatives to match their needs in line with your business priorities.

Top tips

- ❖ **Ask rather than tell - always!**
- ❖ **Communicate more and find out that's going on and what they need.**
- ❖ **Monitor absence and support the employee where you can.**
- ❖ **Engage with the EAP programme to support employees during difficult times.**
- ❖ **Consider employees' work-life balance and encourage them to switch off when they are off.**
- ❖ **Encourage fun and social connections at work.**
- ❖ **Ask your team what is important to them in relation to morale.**

14 THE END

Keep a comprehensive paper trail
throughout the process.

The employment relationship can end for many reasons. The most common are when the employee resigns or retires; other occasions include termination by the employer due to a contract expiring, failure to pass probation, redundancy or dismissal due to the disciplinary process.

The paper trail

Common to all of these scenarios is the key principle of ensuring that you **keep a comprehensive paper trail throughout the process.**

If you terminate an employee's contract of employment, you need to ensure it is done fairly and legally. Often managers do not realise the possible implications of an unfair or constructive dismissal case: the potential cost to the company can be up to 2 year's salary in compensation or reinstatement or re-engagement for the employee if they are successful in their claim. So tread carefully when it comes to termination.

Types of termination

Contract expiry

Ensure the contract you gave the employee is clear regarding when it will end - for example, if it is a specific purpose contract, it should say "at the end of the maternity cover but not longer than one year from the start date".

If an employee's contract is due to expire, ensure that you give them lots of notice in advance of same to confirm their contract will not be renewed. This ensures they are clear and are not expecting it to be extended.

Failed to pass probation

Probation is designed to allow you to assess the employee's overall suitability to the role. If they are not performing to the required level during probation, it is very unlikely they will improve after their probation is over. So give them feedback (see **Chapter 9**) and call it early. Don't wait for the last few weeks of their probation to tell them you are not happy with their performance.

Redundancy

If redundancy is being considered, it is important to start the communication, consultation and engagement process with the employee early. Ask them to help identify alternatives to the potential of redundancy. Listen to and explore any options they present and show that you have considered these options before making a decision to progress the process of redundancy.

Remember it's the role, not the person, that is being made redundant. If there is no other option but to make the role redundant, then you need to identify whether there are other roles available for the employee. Again, ask them for their input into this process.

Take the time required to ensure you have given the process due consideration and keep a detailed paper trail through the process to show you fully engaged and consulted with the employee involved.

Disciplinary

If you need to terminate an employee due to a breach in their contract of employment as a result of invoking and using the disciplinary procedure, reread **Chapter 11** and follow the process carefully and in line with your company policy.

Retirement

Plan the employee's retirement well in advance of the date of retirement.

If the employee is happy to retire, then you should try to help them prepare for their retirement and support them in any way you can.

If the employee challenges their retirement, then you are obliged to objectively justify why they must retire at a specific age. This requires engagement and consultation with the employee.

Resignation

Always ask the employee for their resignation in writing. Add it to your employee records when you receive it. Now schedule their exit interview.

Exit interviews

When an employee has decided to leave, you need to find out why they reached this decision and learn from it. An exit interview can be a great opportunity to get feedback about what is working (or not working) in your organisation and where improvements could be made.

In some cases, their decision to leave may be due to an issue that you as the employer may have an obligation to endeavour to resolve - whether it's a grievance with a colleague or unfair treatment they feel aggrieved about. In other cases, the decision may be due to terms and conditions, which you may be in a position to resolve if you wish to retain the staff member.

The exit interview should take place face-to-face so that responses can be explored when given. **The objective is to gather information that can be turned into actions.**

Explain to the employee the reasons for the exit interview and that the information that is gained will be used for organisational improvements.

Always end the interview on a positive note.

Key questions to ask during an exit interview include:

What are your reasons for leaving the business?

Any other reasons? Anything related to the organisation that encouraged you to make the move?

What are the positive aspects from your time with us?

What did you think of the interview and induction process?

Do you think your role was outlined to you effectively at induction?

Do you have suggestions for areas we could improve on?

What does your new organisation offer that made the role appeal to you?

What can you say about communication within the organisation / your department?

How would you describe the culture or 'feel' of the organisation?

Did you feel like you were an intrinsic part of the organisation's goals, mission, and vision?

Were you developed / inducted adequately for your role(s)?

Did you feel that the training you received was appropriate?

What else would you liked to have received training in during your employment?

> **How well do you think the appraisal system worked for you?**
>
> **What are the key skills and traits we should look for in your replacement?**
>
> **Would you consider working for us again if the situation were right?**

Consider the exit interview as part of your approach to talent management. Former staff should remain as part of your network, where possible, as you may want them to recommend your company as a great place to work to other potential candidates in the future.

Review the information from the interview with a view to implementing changes.

Giving references

When giving a reference, limit the information to the facts and ensure the reference is based on objective criteria - for example, you can't say the employee had a bad attitude unless you can back that up with a performance management paper trail.

Many companies' policy on references limits the number of people who can give employee references. Some limit the information to just the job title and a statement of dates the employee worked with the company.

However, you want to do all you can to have a positive relationship with the employee so it's generally best to give the reference as required, always ensuring the information is based on accurate facts.

Top tips

❖ **Be careful, due to the risk involved, if you are terminating an employee's contract for any reason.**

❖ **Ensure you get every employee's resignation in writing.**

❖ **Follow the process in relation to termination and keep a detailed paper trail.**

❖ **Do an exit interview with all employees and put an action plan in place based on the feedback you glean.**

15 YOURSELF

Ask the same questions of yourself as
you ask your employees in
performance review meetings.

Taking time out to assess your own personal development and being self-aware is really important for your business, your career, your personal success and for self-fulfilment.

Asking the same questions of yourself as you ask your employees in performance development meetings helps you take stock of the personal development goals you need to put in place for yourself.

Self-assessment

The American writer Ralph Waldo Emerson said: "What lies behind us and what lies before us are small matters compared to what lies within us". Self-awareness and self-assessment involves taking a helicopter view and requires a fair assessment of how you are performing. It is also useful to ask people in your work and home setting for their input to get a holistic view. Consider exercise, work-life balance, time management, and training, as well as your people management skills.

Ask yourself these questions and answer them honestly:

> **What is going well?**
>
> **What needs to be improved?**
>
> **What SMART goals will I set for myself?**
>
> **Have I any other goals that I need to achieve?**

Personality

What are your underlying personality traits? There are lots of behavioural and occupational personality assessment tools on the market to help you assess your own personal style.

The better you know yourself, the more proactive you can be in understanding your natural tendencies and underlying personality traits and productivity style. You will come to understand how they impact on how you manage people and how your management style affects the people you work with and your relationships with them.

It is important to note **there is no right or wrong personality; approach or style**. What you need to do is to understand your style and that of the teams you work with.

For example, Maggie might prefer to approach a project differently to you but your job is to help her do it any way that suits her style once it meets the deadline and standards required related by the project. You do not need to micro-manage her approach and it doesn't need to be the same as yours. Learn to accept that everyone is different and that there is no one right way to get things done.

Knowing your traits and other people's traits helps you to modify and adapt your behaviour to suit them and to get the most out of them. A lot of great managers do this without even thinking but all managers need to be aware of it.

Emotional intelligence

Emotional intelligence - sometimes labelled 'social intelligence' - is a core skill for managers and key to success in managing people and progressing your career in organisations. It is described as a person's ability to respond to emotions - of others as well as one's own - and to connect with people emotionally.

Emotional Intelligence involves self-awareness, managing emotions, motivating oneself, empathy and the ability to handle relationships. In today's business environment, **emotional intelligence is considered a vital ingredient in leading your employees.** Good emotional awareness leads to improved staff interaction in the workplace, promotes trust and integrity in the workplace and can assist your organisation in retaining talent in the long-term.

The first step in emotional intelligence is to become aware of emotions, which can be perceived from the voice, face or the body. To be mindful and able to perceive these emotions accurately is a starting point for achieving a good understanding of emotions. Non-verbal emotions include expressions on the face such as happiness, sadness, anger, disgust and fear. These expressions and emotions are universally recognised and can help bridge cultural and language barriers. Body language and the tone, pitch and volume of your voice are other telling factors of your emotions.

Emotions play a huge part in the actions and creativity used daily in the workplace. Stimulating emotional input in the workplace can direct thinking towards the aspects of the business that are of most importance.

Moral intelligence and body intelligence have also been identified as important factors in successful leadership.

Moral intelligence has four main virtues:

- ❖ Integrity.
- ❖ Compassion.
- ❖ Responsibility.
- ❖ Forgiveness.

Body intelligence involves monitoring your body's signals during the working day. Watching your health, weight, what you eat and maintaining an active lifestyle all have a positive effect on your body and in turn on your business performance.

Stress can be harmful, so it is important to be armed with tools to help you relieve stress in difficult situations.

Time management and productivity

We covered the importance of time management earlier. Understanding how you work and identifying how you and your team can increase productivity and efficiency is a process that requires ongoing review and improvement. **Do a time audit** and assess how you can improve your own time and productivity.

Networking

Consider networking opportunities that might benefit your personal development.

Value your time; it's easy to go to network or development sessions and return not sure whether you got anything out of them. If you value your time and are focused on return on your time investment, you are much more likely to get some key learnings you can transfer into action from the event.

Surround yourself with people who make you hungry for life, touch your heart and nourish your soul.

Work-life balance

Rest and time out have an extremely positive effect on overall performance. Down-time, play-time or enjoying hobbies such as music, sports or art also have a positive effect on your performance and productivity.

So take time out from work to engage yourself in your interests and hobbies and to spend with your family and friends.

Harness the power of positivity

Being positive is contagious. Positivity is an essential skill that builds resilience and affects the overall team's performance. It is important in relation to your own belief in yourself, your skills, your knowledge and your outlook. It's also important in terms of your interactions with your team.

Negativity is a waste of time and effort – if there are issues put them on the table and deal with them. Nip issues in the bud if you feel members of your team are being negative.

Positivity, to me, is a core competence. Every business needs to recruit employees who possess positivity as it is a core value of any organisation's success.

Ask others for their input and feedback

Ask your management team, peers, team, mentor and others for their input into your personal development. Consider doing 360-degree feedback. The more feedback you get, the more beneficial it will be for you and for the overall organisation.

Top tips

❖ **Know yourself. Enjoy the journey.**

❖ **Emotional intelligence is a core skill you need to develop on an ongoing basis.**

❖ **Get feedback from others to help you identify your personal development plan.**

16 YOUR PLAN

Your personal development is an
investment in your career.

People management involves being a good manager and requires ongoing personal development to enhance and develop your own skills. **Learn to know yourself - honestly and objectively.**

Your personal development action plan

It's often said that what got you here, won't get you there. Identify what you need to work on and develop to get you to the next step in your career. Learning is a life-long process so ensure you continually have a development plan in place. And remember that what gets measured gets done and gets improved, so use a personal development action plan to spur you into action!

Consider the skills, knowledge and behaviours you need to work on to improve and enhance. Ask yourself these questions:

> **What am I doing well?**
>
> **What can I do better?**
>
> **What will I start doing?**
>
> **What will I stop doing?**
>
> **What will I keep doing?**
>
> **What other points should I note?**

What do you need to do to make this happen? For example, training, mentoring, attending a conference; reading a book ... you decide. Be SMART in your goals.

When are you going to review your progress? You need to schedule review time into your diary to review your personal development as this is an investment in your career.

PERSONAL DEVELOPMENT PLAN			
Question	**Assessment**	**Action Required**	**By When**
What am I doing well?			
What can I do better?			
What will I start doing?			
What will I stop doing?			
What will I keep doing?			
Any other points to note?			

Keep raising the bar

Encourage idea generation and solution-focused problem-solving by asking the right questions. Generate new ideas by getting all the thoughts / problems / solutions / innovations out on the table to see what are all the options *via* brainstorming, mind mapping, etc. Then do an analysis of the strengths and weaknesses or areas for development to go with each idea to help identify the best options that deserve further consideration.

Be open to one idea leading you to another - and then yet another. Sometimes, just getting all your thoughts down on paper will lead you to a conclusion you didn't even know you were looking for.

There are no rules except this: there are no bad ideas in brainstorming, who knows where it will lead?

Your job in the process is to **ask the right questions to encourage curiosity, blue sky thinking, brainstorming and solution-focused problem-solving**.

You need to get your team and yourself thinking outside the box by asking the right thought-provoking questions. Blue sky thinking encourages asking ground-breaking questions with no barriers. You need your employees to do this more often through your guidance *via* asking great questions.

You need to encourage innovation, creativity and ideas and motivate your team to be focused on continuous improvement and new possibilities.

Here are some questions you could consider:

What are the future trends in our sector?

What is our unique selling point from a customer perspective?

What problems do customers have that we are not solving?

What are our customer's pain points?

What could we do better or differently to enhance our operation?

What are we doing now that is not efficient?

What controls do we need to enhance the quality of our systems?

Can we replace what we do now via technology?

Can we enhance what we do now via technology?

What are our competitors doing better?

What are the boundaries?

If you remove the current barriers, what's possible? **The sky is the limit.**

Remember you don't need all the answers. You just need to ask your team and yourself the right questions and take the time to really maximise the potential available to you *via* the knowledge and insight these questions will give you. Then consider the next best step to take.

Top tips

❖ **Set a realistic plan for personal development.**

❖ **Consider skills, knowledge and behaviours.**

❖ **Get input from others in helping you identify what you should include in your personal development plan - accept the feedback graciously.**

❖ **Agree a SMART personal development plan to ensure it will become a reality.**

❖ **Review and reassess progress regularly.**

❖ **Keep raising the bar by scheduling time to focus on development and innovation.**

❖ **Ask open questions and ensure everyone is clear that there are no bad ideas / solutions.**

❖ **The sky is the limit when it comes to ideas - if you encourage people to think outside the box to solve problems and find new innovations.**

17 CONCLUSION

You need a wish bone to dream the dream.

You need a back bone to work hard to make it happen.

And you need a funny bone to enjoy the journey of life.

My grandfather was the source of the little poem on the previous page. He was an amazing person - very wise and a real gentleman.

As a people manager, you need to help your employees to feel part of the vision and dream that your organisation is trying to achieve. You need to know their personal development and career aspirations and dreams. You need to work hard, ensuring your team are doing the right things most effectively to achieve the organisation's goals, while also creating a fun and positive work environment that everyone enjoys.

As a people manager, when you encounter an HR issue - for example, poor performance, high turnover of staff or a number disciplinary cases - remember that what you see may only be a symptom of a bigger issue. You always need to explore and fix the root cause.

Also it's important not to automatically blame the employee. There's an old saying that, when you point a finger at someone, three of your fingers are pointing back at yourself. Consider what your part in the problem may be. What are you doing wrong? For example, you may not be coaching or supporting the employee adequately or appropriately.

And finally, when you put a corrective action in place, learn from it. Doing something wrong is not a mistake - not learning from it is!

I hope you have enjoyed your journey with me as you read this book. My experience has led me to believe that, as a people manager, you don't need to know all the answers but to get the right answer, you do need to ask the right questions. Asking the right questions and having time and space to give employees the opportunity to be heard and really listening are key to positive communication and engagement. Maximising an employee's talent and giving them the opportunity to shine is great for your employees; it's also great for your personal and business success so ensure you put the time and effort into managing your best resource – your team!

I hope you have found some action points you can put into use to help you along your people management journey.

Overall top tips

- ❖ **Questions are the best way to move from what you don't know to what you need to know.**

- ❖ **Always give praise in public but only give constructive feedback in private.**

- ❖ **What is not said often says as much as what is said.**

- ❖ **Emotional intelligence is a vital ingredient in leading your employees.**

- ❖ **If you can't prove it, it never happened!**

- ❖ **Being too busy is the biggest barrier to time management.**

- ❖ **Hiring is probably the most important job you do.**

- ❖ **Employee motivation is key to individual performance, group productivity and maintaining a pleasant work environment.**

- ❖ **Feedback should always be specific and future-focused.**

- ❖ **Nothing must be dealt with immediately but everything must be dealt with correctly.**

- ❖ **Follow your company's procedures and process during the employment journey – consistently!**

- ❖ **A clear, understandable and achievable plan is key to cascading and communicating tasks and responsibilities to all members of staff.**

❖ **Encourage employees to manage their work-life balance.**

❖ **Consider the exit interview part of your approach to talent management.**

❖ **Taking time out to assess your own personal development and being self-aware is really important for your business, your career, your personal success and for self-fulfilment.**

❖ **Enjoy the journey!**

CAROLINE McENERY

Caroline McEnery is Managing Director of **The HR Suite** and an HR & Employment Law Expert.

Caroline speaks and trains on the area of employment law, mediation and other relevant HR related topics.

She has completed a Master's in Human Resources at the University of Limerick, she is CIPD accredited as well as being a trained mediator.

Caroline had worked across various areas of HR for over 20 years in Kerry Group and in the retail and hospitality sector, where she was the Operations & HR Director of the Garvey Group, prior to setting up The HR Suite in 2009.

She is a lead mentor on the ACORNS programme which promotes entrepreneurship for women and a member of the Going for Growth and the Continuing the Momentum entrepreneurship programmes.

Caroline is a member of the Low Pay Commission and an adjudicator in the Workplace Relations Commission.

Caroline speaks widely and writes articles and papers on thought leadership in relation to the future landscape of HR and the challenges and opportunities that it presents for employers and employees.

Maria Walsh, Caroline McEnery, Norah Casey and Gavin Duffy at the Dublin launch of **The Art of Asking the Right Questions.**

THE HR SUITE

The HR Suite offers specialist tailored and effective human resources and business solutions to clients throughout Ireland. We have four key departments: Human Resource Management, Employment Law, Training and Recruitment.

Services provided range from the drafting of employment contracts, data protection obligations, case management and legal representation at all the employment law forums, including the Workplace Relations Commission and the Labour Court. We also handle NERA audits, employee assistance programmes (EAP), investigations and mediation. We provide cost-effective solutions that allow you focus on your core business, while we pro-actively manage your HR activity.

Based in Kerry, with an office in Dublin and a nationwide client base of SMEs and multinationals, The HR Suite has been growing steadily over the last six years. The company now has over 400 clients throughout Ireland and employs a team of HR advisors and recruitment consultants.

Contact **The HR Suite** at:

www.thehrsuiteonline.com

info@thehrsuiteonline.com

Facebook, LinkedIn, Instagram, Twitter

Kerry 066 710 2887

Dublin 01 901 4335

THE Hr SUITE

FOR PEOPLE AND BUSINESS